A
Beautiful
Exchange

Responding to God's Invitation for More

By MEGAN NILSEN

A Beautiful Exchange
Responding to God's Invitation for More
by Megan Nilsen

Printed in the United States of America.

ISBN 9781498437233

www.xulonpress.com

"In every century only a few so earnestly pursue the Lord Jesus Christ. But there are always a few, and they are the ones who keep lit the pathway for those who will come after them."

— *Frank Laubach*, Practicing His Presence

Dedication:

I dedicate this book to all those who bravely walk this
journey of faith, lighting the way for the rest of us. Your
bold responses to God's call inspire me
to follow suit.

Also, to those I desperately love, the ones who link
arms with me on the journey
— Scott, Reese, Brynn, Kelel & Senait.

Without you, there would be no story.

Acknowledgments

There are many people I'd like to thank because, had it not been for their constant prodding and words of support, I never would have had the nerve to enter my leg of the race in the bigger story, let alone write about it.

— My college sweetheart turned one-of-a-kind husband, Scott. There is no better traveling companion. Thank you for graciously and enthusiastically holding down the fort so I could pursue my dream.

— My children who embody the beautifully blended, ever-unique pieces of my heart-walking-around-outside-my-body: Reese, Brynn, Kelel & Senait. Thank you for graciously giving me the space to write, even if it meant take-out for dinner and infinitely more screen-time than your micro-managing mommy would normally allow. Thank you for "chilling me out." You all inspire me every day!

— My ever-loving, all smiles, butt-kicking spiritual coach, Linda Meyer. You basically gave me no choice but to write. Your firm and gentle push was exactly what I needed to actually put pen to paper and turn a dream into a reality.

— My tribe of insanely gorgeous Jesus sisters. This journey is more exciting, beautiful and worth pursuing because you're in it. Not to mention, it's filled with a heck of a lot more laughs!

— My initial cheerleaders and pro-bono editors: Scott, Kirkie, Cassie, Michelle and Ty. Your feedback made this final package readable and, dare I say, enjoyable? (I certainly hope so!) To the one I paid, Renee Nyen, thank you for wisely and lovingly tearing the first draft apart so I could see the potential that lay beneath.

— My "She Speaks" champion, Courtney DeFeo, who wiped my tears after the sting of rejection and essentially told me I was a writer, so I'd better get over myself and get back to work.

— My faithful band of blog buddies who punctured my words with enough supportive comments over the years that gave me the courage to put one foot in front of the other and just keep on writing. I am grateful you read even one word.

— My artist-peeps extraordinaire: Marvin Harrell, Jesus lover and gifted artist, for translating the desires of my heart and designing this gorgeous book cover, and Katie Brase, talented photographer, sister and friend for enduring a Nilsen family photo shoot and basically pulling a rabbit out of a hat to make us all look good. Thank you both, for blessing me with your talents!

— My birth family: my mom, dad and sister, Katie. I don't take for granted that I got to grow up wrapped in your loving arms.

— My Ethiopian children's birth family. You live forever and always in our hearts.

Endorsements

"*As a lifelong 'yes' woman, I adore this book. Megan is a gifted writer who describes the beauty of saying* yes *to God's plan for your life. Not necessarily a* yes *to something good or easy, but a* yes *to Him. Her story is about trust and a motivation to say* yes *to my Father more often.*

'*A Beautiful Exchange' is a book for every person that wants to say* yes, *but fears the other side of obedience. Megan's writing is a gift. She is able to bring her God story to life in a way that makes us yearn for more. Megan's story encourages me to keep seeking God's unique plan for my life.*

'*A Beautiful Exchange' makes this 'yes' girl want to reevaluate her decisions. It's a powerful moment when your* yes *meets God's story and plan. Her* yes *was directly in line with God's purpose for her life–and the result is inspiring.*"

— Courtney DeFeo, Author *In This House We Will Giggle*, Creator of ABC Scripture Cards, Founder @lillightomine

"*Having witnessed this story unfold before me, I saw the irresistible love of God wooing Megan to not only want His will, but to walk in His way. It is a story that confirms that God is good, and great, and oh, so surpassingly surprising!*"

— Rev. Dr. Sara Singleton

"'A Beautiful Exchange' takes the reader into the personal ministry of adoption with a new best friend as guide. Megan Nilsen's transparency and humor is wonderfully balanced with her courageous heart for God and his children. Her friend-next-door voice and loving heart make it nearly impossible to put down. I love this God-honoring, uplifting book."

— Kim de Blecourt, Speaker, Advocate and Author of *Until We All Come Home: A Harrowing Journey, a Mother's Courage, a Race for Freedom*

"'A Beautiful Exchange' is a story of courage, vulnerability and changing hearts, poignantly written in a way that will keep you wanting more — more of Megan's story and more of God in your own life. This book shares compelling insights for those who want to answer God's calling for their own lives."

— Courtney Westlake, Author of the children's book, *That's How You Know* and popular blogger @blessedbybrenna

"In a fresh departure from stories that predictably wrap up in a tidy bow, 'A Beautiful Exchange' is like a fresh cup of water. Megan skillfully tells a story of purpose, pain, and prayer. She leads us to an authentic exchange of hope."

Gari Meacham, Author and Speaker, *Spirit Hunger, Watershed Moments, Truly Fed*

"This book met me in my own story — outside the parameters of adoption — in the first few pages. Nilsen writes with a unique, contemporary style, meeting head on the issues and questions quietly pondered by many in our generation. What does it mean to truly say, 'Send me?' Laced with grace and humor, this is a voice that needs to be heard."

Jill Lynn Buteyn, Author of *Falling for Texas* (Love Inspired) and *Just Show Up* (David C. Cook, due for publication 10/2015)

Table of Contents

In the Beginning, Once Upon a Time and All That Jazz...

"When one has struck some wonderful blessing that all mankind has a right to know about, no custom or false modesty should prevent him [or her!] from telling it, even though it may mean the unbarring of his soul to the public gaze... How I wish, wish, wish that a dozen or more persons who are trying to hold God endlessly in mind would all write their experiences so that each would know what the other was finding as a result! The results, I think, would astound the world. At least the results are astounding to me."

— *Frank Laubach, missionary to the Philippines*

My given name is Megan (no pseudonym here) and I've been a Christian since I could hold a crayon. Now that I'm officially "over-the-hill" plus a couple, it is safe to say I've known *about* God for quite some time. However, it wasn't until recently that I really got to know Him, not just in my head, but in my heart; when God invited me on an intimate journey of revelation and discovery. This God-hewn journey led me (many times kicking and screaming) to the very end of myself, but it also guided me to a place for which I am so thankful, a place I never imagined. This journey ushered me deeper into the heart of God. (I hesitate to use past tense here because, in some ways, the journey is only just beginning...)

The heavenly invitation to embark on such an adventure didn't arrive by snail mail or paperless post. No, the invitation I received felt more like a slight shift in the air. At the time, life as I knew it clicked by at a fairly regular pace. Laundry needed folding, the fridge needed filling and my family needed tending, but when I paused the proverbial treadmill and lifted my face toward heaven, it seemed like the atmosphere just smelled...different...like precious oil anointing a new season. I couldn't put my finger on the details, but I sensed something was about to change.

The intimate reverberations of a still, small voice beckoned me closer. Closer to wholeness, closer to my destiny and, most alluringly, closer to God. He wanted to take me on a faith journey that promised to break every law of control I had so carefully manufactured.

It seems that over the years, whether knowingly or unknowingly, I have made alliances with counterfeit truth:

-   Truth masquerading as the importance of outward appearance — I believed beauty was in the eye of the beholder and the beholder set the standard.
-   Truth disguised as the dogma of worldly success — I figured there was a certain ladder to climb and gosh darn it, I would find it.
-   Truth manifested in the opinions of others — I cared what other people thought and, consequently, made decisions accordingly, for better or for worse.

The Christian cliché of living for an "audience of one" often felt more like a New Year's resolution than an attainable reality.

I understand full well that life's trajectory can change in the blink of an eye. One phone call, one ambush from an invisible patch of black ice, or a terminal diagnosis; these things can change a life forever — but so can an intimate encounter with the God of the Universe. Saying *yes* to a divine invitation can change your life. It did mine.

Heaven knows I love a good meal. My heart is all kinds of happy when I'm sitting in a quiet corner booth with my hubby on a Saturday night, dreaming about our future together and what we'll "share" for dessert. I am deliriously grateful enjoying a margarita on the rocks relishing nachos and belly laughs with my "besties." But oh, these worldly pleasures sit on the tip of the iceberg of what true life can actually be.

Is the phrase, "on earth as it is in heaven," just a rote recitation chanted in unison cadence on a Sunday morning? Or is it something God longs to lavish on His children as a present promise? Could it be that one of God's deepest desires is to awaken our hearts to the reality that He wants us to experience the vast height, depth and breadth of His love not simply when we're called home to heaven, but here and now?

What if God wants us to experience something more than a weekly church service or a daily quiet time? If we make the time to slow down and really take it all in, we just might realize that the deepest parts of Him are calling out to the deepest parts of us. If it's true, if Jesus came to give life to the full (John 10:10), what might that look like for you and for me?

I feel like an explorer on a quest for buried treasure, and I'm fairly certain the treasure for which I search holds the keys to the Kingdom of God — a Kingdom that separates perceived truth from what is *most* true. All is not necessarily as it seems. Jesus himself warned us not to judge *"by appearances, but judge with right judgment,"* (John 7:24, ESV). He offers a Kingdom unlike anything this world can offer — full of refreshing salve for the deepest of wounds, redemption for the broken, freedom for the oppressed and recovery of sight for the blind — a Kingdom more beautiful and valuable than the rarest jewel.

I operated with limited sight for much too long — making decisions based on the appearance of things in shadows, flickers of silhouettes cast upon a wall. Make no mistake, however; I do not pity my former self. I was and am redeemed and called by name (Isaiah 43:1), loved and guided by Jesus, lo these many years. My Heavenly Daddy patiently nurtured my unassuming heart all along the way. After all, shadows only exist in the presence of Light.

However, things are different now. There is a call to live, a call to explore, a call to receive and worship in the unique, custom-made way my Creator wove deep into my DNA. Perhaps you find yourself in a similar spot — hungry and restless, eager to bust out of the box and live a bigger story. A story that changes the world around you because it changes *you*.

The details and circumstances of your life may mirror my own or portray a vastly different reality as you sit in a time or place, a culture or generation different from mine. May I boldly suggest those details are irrelevant? Though our individual lives are wonderfully unique, the deeper truths for God's beloved children are universal. God's invitation to journey into a more authentic relationship with Him and, in turn, with those around us remains the same.

Do you find yourself on a mysterious and confusing journey? Or maybe you sense God calling you to enter one? Either way, the divine truths God revealed to me in the boots-on-the-ground living of this beautifully, messy adventure of faith is one that, I believe, can only be unpacked in the pages of a book. A book penned by an ordinary woman, living an ordinary life. The thing is, I am (just as you are) loved by no ordinary God!

So it begins.

Or, so it began...

Several years ago, a whisper turned into a call and I am not the same.

Smack in the summer of our 14th year of marriage, Scott and I came face to face with the Holy of Holies. Ironically, nothing particularly extraordinary had transpired. In fact, it was quite the opposite. We were college sweethearts turned late-thirty-something couple, raising a family in Western America; a boy and a girl and a yellow lab (not necessarily in that order). Our life looked like that of so many others. From a worldly perspective, we had it all. Perhaps that was precisely the problem. Though we had everything we ever wanted, we couldn't shake the thought that there had to be more to the story — more to *our* story.

What were we missing? We didn't know the answer to these questions, but God planted a restlessness in our hearts and we wanted to find out why. We didn't necessarily make any radical decisions in order to do so. We didn't downsize or scale back or quit anything per se. We simply committed to slow down and lower the volume of extraneous noise in our lives. From the vantage point of two people on our knees, we implored God to exchange our conservative, worldly view for a life filled with heaven's divine plan so we could live the story we were made to live — one drafted by His own hand. You know the strangest thing? We didn't have to wait long for an answer.

In the midst of our natural, ordinary, everyday suburban kind of life, we sensed our hearts stir at the gentle breath of a holy whisper. Over the years we'd felt the winds of change, the shifts of season, but this breeze felt different, as if uniquely created and packaged just for us in the heavenly realms. This supernatural current carried with it an invitation to follow the Lord into what felt to us like uncharted territory. God extended His hand and beckoned us to follow Him on a journey that promised to unveil a brand new vantage point in the Kingdom of Heaven — a way to experience Him and explore His heart in new ways.

God set a vision before us that would shatter the closely monitored paradigm we had so carefully crafted for ourselves. He knew in order to *really* change us, He needed to reach deep inside our hearts and weave His Spirit into a most intimate and valued place — our family. He invited us to consider the journey of adoption.

The invitation to grow our family in this way painted a picture of a story larger than the four of us, one that bore the signature markings of risk and adventure and heart palpitations. However, even amidst all the immediate questions of *who, what, when, where, how,* and *why-on-earth-us*, we couldn't deny this invitation carried a profound promise that we would encounter the heart of God in a whole new way.

What seemed like an unnatural leap of faith presented an even greater offer if we chose to accept it. When tucked in the favor of the Lord's hand, could something so seemingly *unnatural* become a kind of *holy natural*? If the Lord's blessing was on this call, then more than anything, we wanted to follow. We didn't make any overnight decisions; we figured we'd pray about it first.

Admittedly, we didn't hear the *audible* voice of God in response to our prayers, but the impression the Holy Spirit seared on our hearts felt undeniable. We knew if we didn't at least *see* where this road might lead we would, in effect, be saying "no" to God. Our hearts were not settled with that. Not knowing all the answers, unable to map the course with any certainty, we closed our eyes, locked our fingers in white knuckle formation and offered words that went something like this, *"Here we are, Lord. Send us. In this way, at this time, we will obey your call."*

Indeed, the Lord had spoken to us but, fearing the life we had so carefully manufactured for ourselves might very well look like a barren stump at the end of it all; did we *really mean* what we just said? In his book, *Surprised by the Voice of God*, author Jack Deere shares an important revelation about how God speaks to His people:

> *The clearer the revelation, the harder the task. God gave the Israelites the Ten Commandments with the clarity of an audible voice because keeping the commands of a holy God would be the most difficult task that the nation of Israel would ever face. When God speaks in an audible voice, you can be sure the powers of hell will rise up to challenge that voice. When God speaks to you most clearly, it usually means you are going to go through such a difficult experience that later you will need to be absolutely certain that God has spoken to you. In fact, the clarity of the voice may be the main thing that gives you the power to endure the subsequent testing.*

God invited us to exchange our ways for His ways, our thoughts for His thoughts, our preconceived plans for His heavenly purposes. Ultimately, the exchange that was about to take place would be more beautiful than we could ever imagine. However, when we found ourselves lost and wandering in a spiritual wilderness 18 months later, Deere's words proved to be most prophetic indeed.

Chapter 1:

"God, Send Me" and Other Things We Might Not *Really* Mean

"And I heard the voice of the Lord saying, 'Whom shall I send, and who will go for us?' Then I said, 'Here am I! Send me.'"

— *Isaiah 6:8, ESV*

I sat at the McDonald's play place, amidst splotches of ketchup and scattered chicken nuggets, wondering how *this* had become my new sanctuary. A location I previously avoided like the plague (mostly because I was certain that is exactly what my children would contract if they played there) was now an oasis of sorts. The small windowed room, filled with a few square tables bolted to the floor and a web of red and yellow tunnels, provided the stimulation my two extremely active, newly adopted Ethiopian children needed in that moment. Not to mention, it boasted the added benefit of being confined within four walls so neither child could attempt to escape my watchful eyes, which were weary and mediocre at best.

21

In the early days of our time home as a freshly formed family of six, most of my friends knew to pick up the phone immediately when my number appeared on the screen. They realized the caller was most likely trying to get through to a member of her crisis hotline team. Annie just happened to live closest to the preferred (a.k.a. least gnarly) play place so she grew to expect my calls.

"Hey," she'd answer. "You doing okay?"

"Uh, yeah. Well, no...I don't know. I just need to get out of the house and these kids need to burn off some serious energy."

"I'm guessing you're ready for another round of French fries and a listening ear. We're loading up. See you in twenty minutes!"

On the drive over, I glanced in the rearview mirror at the beautiful and confused ebony children in the backseat and pondered just how in the world all this had come to pass – that strangers from vastly different parts of the world had just morphed into one family. I wondered how following God's heart in this way translated into me basically jumping over the fast food counter to point at the menu screen in order to determine exactly *which* sandwich, hamburger or milkshake this non-English speaking seven year old boy desperately wanted.

"Number 8? Number 6? Number 5?" I turned his face toward the overwhelming and brightly lit screen. "Which... picture...do...you...like?!"

My son's incoherent grunts and wild eyes didn't steer me in any clear direction. I picked one and paid. Apparently I got it wrong. I tried again. Surely he'll like at least *one* of these things, I reasoned. When we finally made our way into the play zone, Annie's kids took over. They graciously guided mine down plastic slides and back up again. In a virtual daze, I sat with my friend and murmured, "So – this is what it looks like to follow God, eh? What it feels like to take the Bible seriously… I sure hope I can be the mom these kids need. I have *no clue* how to do this."

There are some Bible verses that get a lot of mileage in Christian circles. Certainly John 3:16 takes the cake. Kids as young as three-years-old can rattle off "for God so loved the world…" in a moment's notice, making Mama and Daddy smile with combustible pride in the presence of faithful passersby. Frankly, most modern day Americans can at least get close to reciting this one from memory thanks to Tim Tebow's brief rise to fame.

"For I know the plans I have for you declares the Lord, plans to prosper you and not to harm you, plans to give you hope and a future," (Jeremiah 29:11, NIV). That's another good one. Key chains, bookmarks, and cross-stitch art all shine with this verse wherever Christian books are sold. (I didn't even have to look that one up as I typed it just now. Thank you, devoted Sunday school teachers!) What girl doesn't want to build a cabin and stay a while in that comfy universe?

However, there are other verses that don't transport us to such a cozy place. When Jesus touts phrases like, *"Let the dead bury their own dead,"* (Luke 9:60) or, *"Do not think I have come to bring peace to the earth. I have not come to bring peace, but a sword,"* (Matthew 10:34); we often scratch our heads in confusion and flip over to the next palatable verse. We may believe these words to be important in some "inerrancy-of-Scripture" kind of way, but true understanding will only come through revelation of the Holy Spirit. (I would love to see the looks on the judges' faces if a Miss America contestant came back with one of these salty retorts when asked about her desire for world peace! She'd get my vote.)

On the other hand, we have the opportunity to land on certain verses that naturally elevate our blood pressure and elicit spontaneous "Amens!" from even the most stoic of hearts. Olympic athletes tattoo Philippians 4:13 on their ankles, *"I can do all things through him who strengthens me."* Sympathy cards abound with Romans 8:28 embossed in fancy font, *"And we know that for those who love God all things work together for good, for those who are called according to his purpose."* Yes and amen! Truly, these words are water for a parched soul.

The book of Isaiah is chock-full of fantastic, paint-them-on-your-doorframe type verses. I'd personally rank Isaiah 6:8 among the very best, *"And I heard the voice of the Lord saying, 'Whom shall I send, and who will go for us?' Then I said, 'Here am I! Send me.'"* My heart rate spikes at the sight of those words. *"Put me in, Coach! I'm ready to play... today..."* (Those of you in a certain age range are singing the rest of the lyrics right now, aren't you? Yeah, me too.) Such inspiration packed into so few words. Slap that bumper sticker on the back of my SUV and send me on my way.

I came upon this well-known passage at the inception of our adoption process. I was eager to understand God's heart more clearly, and this seemed just the ticket. "Who cares if you're scared out of your mind?" I reasoned. "God wants you in the game, girl." At least that's the message that would ultimately prove to be an anchor to my anxious soul. However, at the end of the day, with all the chips on the table — did I really *mean* it?

There are a lot of amazing Bible verses out there. Truly. However, in that moment, did this verse trump them all? If human beings are crafted in the image of God, it seems perfectly reasonable to assume we are wired to want to make a difference in this world — that we would embody God's heart. Nevertheless, giving up control of exactly *what* that looks like is another story entirely. I wanted God to use me for His Kingdom glory — no doubt — but I was also extremely tempted to draft a proposed blueprint of the plan I envisioned. "Risk free" might very well have been at the top of the list. Was I ready to cash it in and go for broke?

Isaiah 6:8 is a doozy. No longer are we promised grace and forgiveness of sins or a heavenly after party with Jesus. No guarantees of health and prosperity here. Just a call to take up arms and head into battle. Granted, Wonder Woman and Xena: Warrior Princess garner my utmost respect, but was this *really* the path I wanted to pick in my own version of *Choose Your Own Adventure* stories? At the invitation of a loving God, we were about to choose the adventure of adoption and my heart was anything but settled.

I stumbled upon a commentary of this verse on January 14, 2011 while dutifully reading Oswald Chamber's wildly famous devotional book, *My Utmost for His Highest*. I like to think of his book as the yin to Sarah Young's *Jesus Calling* yang. Chambers hits the head while Young tackles the heart. Though I must confess, Oswald's words compel me to whip out my highlighter more often than not when his revelations strike both head and heart in one fell swoop.

Perhaps Ozzy wasn't the life of the party at company dinners in his day. I don't know for sure, but he probably wasn't voted "Class Clown" or "Biggest Flirt." However, I bet he still would have been interesting to sidle up to on a mid-summer's eve. I imagine I would have enjoyed listening to him pontificate for hours. There aren't a lot of witty quips in his writing. Not many LOL, smiley face, exclamation point moments. In fact, most of what he wrote flies well over my head. I don't know anything about his life here on earth, although I'm fairly sure he died at a young age. (Many of the good ones do.) However, more often than not, when God graciously illumines my human mind in a moment of divine encounter, Ozzy's passages pretty much kick my hiney.

Lo and behold, on that day I came upon his written offering and Chambers turned another well-known passage on its head. When I cracked open the pages that chilly January morning, God opened my eyes to something I'd never seen before. Contrary to my pre-conceived beliefs about this section of Isaiah, it turns out God wasn't specifically calling on Isaiah at all. Chambers observes, *"God did not address the call to Isaiah; Isaiah overheard God saying, 'Who will go for us?'* [Now here's the kicker!] *The call of God is not for the special few, it is for everyone. Whether or not I hear God's call depends upon the state of my ears; and what I hear depends upon my disposition."*

In this passage, Isaiah encounters the Holy of Holies. In some truth-is-stranger-than-fiction sci-fi moment, the angels surrounding the Lord cover themselves in reverence and holy fear. They sing of His glory and the whole temple fills with smoke. Isaiah immediately shrinks with the revelation of his profound unworthiness and confesses he is a sinful man. No sooner does Isaiah make this confession than an angel swoops down, touches his lips with a burning coal and declares Isaiah's guilt removed and his sins forgiven. It is only *after* experiencing this profound encounter with grace that Isaiah's ears open and he hears the Lord asking for a volunteer to be a messenger to his people. Isaiah thrusts his hand in the air and in a Shrek and Donkey kind of moment blurts out, "Pick me! Pick me!"

Ahem. I hesitate to pause the story here, but Isaiah, do you even *know* what God is going to ask you to do? Mightn't you inquire before you so pompously volunteer yourself for the mission? My 21st-century, American mind would like to have some more details before I blindly go off into the deep, dark woods all Little-Red-Riding-Hood. What's the return policy? Is my satisfaction guaranteed? What about five-star customer service and creature comforts? Not to mention a 401k or Roth IRA.

In full disclosure, I admit I have followed this same line of questioning in some of my conversations with the Lord. I've unfurled my list of rebuttals expecting well-thought out, comprehensive answers in return. As it turns out, however, the Lord's message via Isaiah is none too pretty. God is about to appoint Isaiah to bona fide prophet status in order to declare the coming of death, destruction and wastelands. Gee, sounds fun. I wouldn't be surprised if his "prophet rating" plummeted big time.

Upon hearing the message, Isaiah asks the Lord how long he must do this. Okay, n*ow* Isaiah is singing my song. Let's put some parameters on this thing! Apparently, it's going to be a while, as God scatters His people to distant lands and the whole blasted country withers into an utter wasteland. Israel will become but a stump. Ha! There it is. I figured there had to be a catch.

Wait a minute, the story isn't over, "...*the stump will be a holy seed that will grow again,*" (Isaiah 6:13). What would be destroyed would be made new. God intended to restore beauty from the ashes. In that moment, I wondered if this story was a metaphor for our family. Was our family life about to turn into a virtual ashtray? We couldn't deny our hearts beat ever stronger in an effort to be allied with something bigger than ourselves but, under the cover of our private thought chamber, we wondered if this choice to follow God was really worth the risk.

In words too raw to share in righteous Christian circles, we wondered, "Really, God? Are you sure you have the right people? We know you're good and you want to take care of each and every sheep in your flock, but how do we know you're really gonna pull through on *this* one? If we take a step off the cliff with you, Jesus, will we free fall or will we fly?" Not to mention, whether we said 'yes' or 'no' to this invitation would have a direct impact on the trajectory of the future of some unsuspecting child (or children) living a vastly different life somewhere in this great big world. Was this God's plan of provision for them? Then there were our two biological kids sleeping peacefully under our roof. How would this decision affect their lives?

As a life-long Christian, I was ashamed I even entertained those thoughts. After all, we had obediently followed God's call in years past – into a life of vocational ministry, into selling our newly built dream home for a job God provided on the other side of the state, into making the decision for me to be a stay-at-home mom while my husband worked. Yes, we had followed His hand in all these things, but this decision felt different. This one felt...permanent. The phrase, *"Here I am, send me,"* carried extra weight as I wound it around all the lives it would impact.

Maybe we meant what we said and maybe we didn't, but we were compelled to walk in the Lord's direction nevertheless. The joy set before us gleamed brilliantly in our mind's eye. We wanted to know Him more deeply, to experience Him more intimately. God had always proved faithful in the past. Who were we to question that now? Not looking to the right or to the left, we took a deep breath, put one foot in front of the other and began to walk in obedience toward the call that came our way which, in our case, included the journey of adoption.

We figured the challenges might overwhelm us and heaven knew our family would never look exactly the same again, but the Lord would prove faithful; of that we were certain. He could and would turn the proverbial stump headed our way into a holy seed that would bloom again.

At least, we hoped.

Chapter 2:

Beach Entry Exploration Outside the "Comfort Zone"

"Lord, if it's you," Peter replied,
"Tell me to come to you on the water."

—Matthew 14:28, TNIV

What prompted us to explore life outside our perceived comfort zone in the first place? We were comfortable little clams nesting in a temperature-controlled environment. As they say, if it ain't broke don't fix it.

Just five years prior, Scott and I tooled along the back roads of Northern California in celebration of our tenth wedding anniversary. The vehicle we rented, complete with satellite XM radio and convertible roof, allowed us to bask in the warm rays of the Golden State sun. Tunes filled the atmosphere as the wind whipped through our hair. We meandered along the sophisticated streets of San Francisco before heading to the lush emerald vineyards of Napa Valley's world-renowned wine country where we soared over the vast landscape in a brilliantly colored hot-air balloon and closed out each night with farm-to-table fare paired with glasses of rich, oaky blends. (Dang, I'm salivating just thinking about it!)

It was precisely on one of those romantic California afternoons, between bites of creamy brie cheese and crispy baguette, that one of us first uttered the "A" word. Adoption.

At the time, our biological children were six and three years old. By all accounts, we were experiencing what we considered the perfect life. As happily married parents of two, we owned a house (or at least a 30-year-fixed loan) and an 80-pound yellow lab and worked for a thriving Christian ministry. Maybe it was the wine talking or perhaps my biological clock, but I decided to take a risk and bring up the oft-dismissed subject of Nilsen family planning. Scott was quite content with the order of events up until this point and, to some degree, so was I. However, in classic Megan fashion, I just couldn't help myself. Before we seriously entertained the idea of surgically altering, rather *halting*, the possibility of adding more cherubic, tow-haired children to our quiver, we probably should be on the same page. That seemed wise if we wanted to live in an equally yoked kind of way.

Scott was soundly of the two kids, "replace yourself" persuasion, and I was too....mostly. I didn't have an easy time postpartum with either of my babies and the memory of returning home at the end of a long work day only to be greeted by a wife who was crying harder than the kids was enough to send him racing to the urologist! No, birthing more biological children didn't seem to be the right answer for our family. If we were to ever have more children — and believe you me, that was a big *if* — we agreed to entertain the idea of adoption. After all, we reasoned, there were (and still are) plenty of kids around the world without a family to care for them for one reason or another. Perhaps we would be asked to step in and fill that role. I could live with that.

There was a certain safety in staying away from the delivery room again and yet, the possibility remained that our family could grow. If a magic stork brought children into our life through (God-forbid) a tragic accident of some sort we would be ready. If a friend of a friend knew of some precious children who had no kin to call their own and thought we would be the perfect family, we would be there, ready to rise to the occasion. Easy. All we had to do was wait. If God had this method of family expansion in the cards for us, we figured it would come to us and if not, then it wasn't meant to be. Simple. Case closed. We would await God's lead.

At fourteen years in, our married-with-kids days clicked away at a rapid pace. Scott's job responsibilities increased a couple of times, we moved to a new city and lived in our potential "forever house." We created family memories left and right. The photo albums filled quickly with pictures of annual birthday parties and extended family Christmas celebrations.

We ticked off the chronological checklist. Both kids finally matriculated in all-day school. Check. First trip to Disneyland. Check. Mom ready to head back to work. Check! The plan seemed to fall into place. Although I *loved* kissing sticky cheeks and wiping stinky bottoms, I dreamed of the day I might re-enter the workforce and become what I deemed a productive member of society again.

The notion of adoption comfortably took a back seat as the daily regimen of school choir concerts, dance recitals and soccer games filled our days. The idea sifted through my mind every so often like sand in an hourglass. My mental to-do list read as follows: don't forget to buy milk, figure out the name of that cool paint color from the Pottery Barn catalogue, and, God, if you ever want us to adopt, just remember our hearts are open. My prayer journal chronicled devotional musings, memory verses and a laundry list of prayer requests for ailing friends or grieving loved ones, followed by the occasional, *"Oh by the way, if you intend for us to adopt a child, could you please write it in the sky or shout it from the rooftop or something? That would be great...Thanks!"* thrown in for good measure.

I did, in fact, go back to work. I accepted the perfect part-time job opportunity as the MOPS (Mothers of Pre-Schoolers) advisor at our local church. Not only did this work prove meaningful, it also provided me the freedom to continue volunteering in my children's classrooms as well as contribute a meager pay check to pad our family expense reports. Life was looking up! Throughout the course of that year, however, I couldn't shake a silent but nagging feeling God had something else in store for me — for us. But what?

The days played out exactly as I had scripted them in my head. Could a possible alternate reality be in the works? I wasn't entirely sure, but I sensed part of the key to finding out what grander plans God might have for our family would be to make more time to pointedly seek Him. That would require time and availability — an openness to move when and if He said move. I knew He was stirring my heart to quit the job for which I had longed. Reluctant, but hopeful, I obeyed.

Just about the time I turned in my resignation at church, some good friends of ours returned home from Ethiopia with a beautiful baby boy. We had walked hand in hand with them through their adoption process and celebrated their safe return home with a bouncing bundle of joy in their arms. "Good for them," we thought. What a beautiful manifestation of God's love. God adopted us into His family and they adopted Joshua Birhanu into theirs — such an amazing completion of this holy circle.

That same month the telephone rang, signaling another jolt to my scattered thoughts.

"Hey, Megan! It's Jill."

"Hi, Jill. Good to hear from you! It's been so long. How's Air Force life treating you?" I spoke over the laughter of children enjoying a game of tag in the cul-de-sac.

"Things are great here in Florida, but we miss you all back in Colorado." She cleared her throat. "I'm actually calling because Scotty and I have an announcement," her voice trailed off.

"Oh, all right...What is it?"

"We wanted to call and let you know we recently started the adoption process to adopt a baby girl from — Ethiopia!"

"Wow. That's, um...amazing. Truly. Congratulations!"

What the what?! I had no idea adoption was on their radar. Two families in two months adopting from Ethiopia — good friends and my cousin and his wife. What were the odds? God's economy continued to grow, muddling the lines between nature and nurture, black and white. The coincidence seemed uncanny. At that point, my mind blurred. Thoughts of previous conversations and flippant phrases uttered over the years like, "I'm not sure if we're done having children. I mean, we might consider adoption or we'd be open to the idea if a situation came our way," rushed into my head. Into my heart. The floodgates cascaded open.

God what are you doing here? I questioned. *I thought we had settled the score on this subject. We were waiting for you to go ahead and just drop this in our laps, remember?*

Okay, okay. Slow down, I reasoned. *No rush here. I'll just continue to pray. No need to be anxious. Maybe I'm over-thinking this.* However, as the days ticked by, I couldn't get the drum beat of these thoughts out of my head. Like a catchy lyric turning over and over in my mind, this idea of adoption, that it might possibly be for us, kept knocking at the door of my heart and wouldn't abate.

One night, while Scott and I prepped for bed, inserted between the brushing and the flossing (always the *perfect* time to bring up a delicate subject with your spouse), I boldly laid it all on the line.

"Hey, babe...I, uh, I have something to tell you."

"Um, okay." He gulped, toothbrush in one hand, iPhone dangling in the other.

In a solitary barrage of thought, the litany of words spewed from my mouth. "I don't need a response. In fact, I don't even want you to say anything right away, I just want you to know I can't get this idea of adoption out of my head. It just keeps coming back and I can hardly think of anything else. I mean, the Martins adopted and now Scotty and Jill...I just...I don't know...I wonder if this is something we're really supposed to consider too?"

Relieved to honor my request for silence, Scott processed the words. To him it felt like I'd just pulled the pin on an incoming grenade, but to me it was a welcome relief to the tension that had gripped my mind over the previous weeks. He absorbed my stream-of-consciousness fire hose and, after a brief silence, with resoluteness of tone, he received my heart.

"You sound...serious. I don't know...I...guess we should pray about it."

My shoulders relaxed. Finally! This was not mine to bear alone. For months and perhaps years, I harbored these thoughts and feelings in my own mind. Now, as it should be, we would be one, praying together for God to reveal His plan for our family. As my eyelids grew heavy, my mind cleared away any extra emotional weight. Scott lay perfectly still, eyes fixed on a dark ceiling.

What had he just agreed to? Where on earth would this crazy journey take us?

We stacked hands on the importance of sharing this vision — this invitation — with Reese and Brynn. A decision of this magnitude would impact the whole family. We respected their feelings and valued their voice in the process. To be clear, there are times when Mom and Dad's decision trumps all. You can lay down a well-placed, "because I said so" when you implore your child for the umpteenth time to cut the crap and get their little behind to bed or refrain from burping the alphabet at the dinner table, but this was not one of those times.

We decided to surprise the kids one evening with a trip to their favorite restaurant. (We may or may not eat out more often than I care to admit, but we played it up nevertheless.) The bubbly hostess grabbed menus and crayons and led us to a corner table for four. As Reese and Brynn challenged each other to multiple games of tic-tac-toe on the butcher paper tablecloth, Scott teed up the ball.

He cleared his throat, "Guys, can I, uh, have your attention?" Nothing. The continuous banter over whose crayon was whose indicated he wasn't getting anywhere. He changed his tactic. "Reese, Brynn — your Mom and I have been discussing the possibility of something *really big* and we want to ask you how you feel about it."

Childlike squeals of victory and groans of defeat faded. Crayons found their way back into the box. Their attention turned to us.

"There is something God has laid on my, well, *our* hearts," I confided. "And we truly want to know how you feel about it because this decision will impact our whole family if we choose to go down this path."

"All right already!" their eyes pleaded.

I stepped in and took the plunge. "We have sensed God's call to *maybe* add a little brother or sister to our family…"

Their suspicious eyes grew wide with embarrassment. "No, not the old fashioned way," I winked. "Through adoption."

Gulp. The words hovered above the table. Would they explode in our faces or land gently on the tarmac of civil family discussion?

To our delight and surprise, it was the latter. Reese and Brynn, though young in age were wise of thought and tender of heart. Always the logician, Reese reasoned if it was, in fact, God's holy invitation, then we should proceed accordingly.

Brynn's compassionate heart burst open with enough love necessary to adopt a dozen children. Whoa, slow down, sister!

Had God gone before us and prepared the way in their hearts as well? We cast the vision and they caught hold. Not only was Scott on board, but the kids followed suit. All of a sudden the idea of adoption wasn't tucked safely in the land of the theoretical; it threatened to transform into a reality. Heaven, help me! I had been the catalyst of this whole thing. I ventured outside the comfort zone of my own thoughts, dipped my toes into unknown waters and, as it turned out, the whole family was in favor of the idea. I had finally said what I meant, but did I really *mean* what I said?

I wonder if Peter felt this way when Jesus invited him to step out of the boat. I didn't want to act *too* impulsively. I preferred to test the waters, maybe pull together a feasibility study. I wanted Jesus to walk right up to me then and there and map out the course or write it in the sky or visit me in a dream! *Anything.* I wasn't a fan of the churning uncertainty.

Now I was the resident insomniac. *Lord Jesus, please help us figure this all out.*

I thought I was ready to dive straight into the deep end, no holds barred, but my family called my bluff. Perhaps I really was more comfortable sitting on the spiritual sidelines, daydreaming about partnering with God for a lost and hurting world, cheering on *other* people who were way more qualified than I. Did I actually have the guts to follow God out onto the field of play?

It was time to put legs on my faith. I sat squarely in my own "come to Jesus" kind of moment. The Lord had invited me to step out of the boat and I suppose I did — at least a little bit. I dipped my toes in the water, tested the temperature and explored the shallow end. It was time to figure out how far I was willing to go. The only problem was that I didn't actually know how to discern the details of such a profound call.

I figured it wouldn't hurt to dig out a couple old Bible studies I'd done over the years, maybe sift through the pages of other people's wisdom. Perhaps I'd uncover guidance from renowned teachers I deeply respected – learn how they discerned God's voice. The results were in and they were largely unanimous. Almost every study suggested I spend time in prayer and engage in moments of solitude and worship. Those actions alone would position me to hear from the Lord. From that posture, I asked God to illuminate His words for me in Scripture. I also humbled myself before some trusted, God-fearing friends and vulnerably requested advice and prayer — not just as a matter of checking off some nice, Christian to-do list, but with a hunger to truly encounter the will of God.

The path was murky at best, but I marched forward in the only way I knew how — one step, one moment, and one revelation at a time.

Chapter 3:

Following God is Like a Box of Chocolates

*"Taste and see that the LORD is good. Oh, the joys
of those who take refuge in him!"*

– Psalm 34:8, NLT

A few weeks after our "Team Nilsen" dinner-date, the dog days of summer faded into fall, signaling the start of a new school year. God's call of adoption lingered like sweet perfume over my heart and mind, but for the life of me I couldn't decide if I really liked the scent. Perhaps adoption was something God intended for *other* people, I reasoned. Maybe it wasn't, you know, for *us*. The insidious indecisiveness lodged deep in my DNA began to annoy even me. The thing I had dreamed of for over five years was finally manifesting in real-time action. As we began to proactively explore options and agencies, I didn't know how to integrate my fickle emotions.

One August morning *(the 23rd to be exact)*, after braving the elementary school drop-off lane with rushed kisses and frantic good-byes, the Holy Spirit nudged me to curtail my plans for the day. A list of errands ran through my mind. I had so much to do. I can't explain it any other way, except to say the to do list felt trite and a holy invitation leapt to the top of the list.

"Scratch your personal plans for the day," the whisper seemed to say. *"Exchange your agenda for mine and meet with me. I have something for you..."*

Work no longer filled my days, so spontaneity was an option. Instead of turning left and heading to the gym, I turned right and headed home. Despite the strong urge to tidy up, I grabbed my Bible and settled in at our sticky kitchen table. The dirty dishes and mounting laundry stared me down like a bull taunting a matador.

Don't get distracted, I commanded myself. *Don't let anything derail your attention. Today is the day to leave it all at the cross. Dive in and ask Jesus to lead. Only then will true answers come.*

God made it clear He wanted me to spend the day in prayer and fasting; searching the Bible to see what *He* had to say on the subject of adoption. I had spent many years asking others and avoiding this type of tender vulnerability with the Lord. If I honestly sought His will for our family, it stood to reason I should spend time *pointedly asking* and, more importantly, *actively listening.* I quieted my ever-active mind and set my heart on Him.

Instead of closing my eyes and randomly pointing to a passage of Scripture in a game of divine darts like I might normally do, I opened up the concordance and referenced the word, "orphan." Those searches alone led me on a full-blown tour of the Holy Scriptures. Straight off the pages of Deuteronomy, God commanded the early Jewish community to remember widows, aliens and orphans in their distress; three oft-forgotten remnants of society. In Psalm 68:5-6, God reveals Himself as a *"father to the fatherless, a defender of widows."* He promises to *"set the lonely in families."*

It should come as no surprise to anyone vaguely familiar with the heart of God that His Word is chock-full of messages regarding His heart for the fatherless. From the beginning of time, God set out to provide companions for his people. He provided Adam with Eve and the body of Christ with the Holy Spirit. Could it be that His plan for our home fell in line with His plan for all of creation? That nobody would be left abandoned or fatherless?

My heart rate accelerated as I transitioned to the New Testament and absorbed Jesus' promise to return to us, His people. He would not leave us as "orphans." He would come in the form of our counselor and guide, the Holy Spirit. Those of us who are Gentiles have a keen perspective into this adoptive community because we were never part of God's chosen people in the first place. Only through the sacrificial blood of our Lord, Jesus Christ, are we graciously grafted into His family, His community, His people. Through this redemptive act of *adoption*, we too can be called, "children of God."

The silent hours passed in a flash as my heart and mind flooded with words and thoughts containing one singular, revolutionary message: *I was an orphan.* At least, in God's economy. In His tender mercy, God chose to adopt me just as He has chosen to adopt you. In this moment, He was inviting our family to put feet on our faith and "go and do likewise." I could hide no longer. The gospel message housed for years in my *mind* finally penetrated my *heart*.

Seated around the dinner table that night, I shared these personal revelations with Scott and the kids. What had previously appeared so complicated now seemed clear and, to be honest, utterly terrifying. Though everyone else was on board with the plan, ironically, I had been the lone holdout. I slowly released my fierce grip on our current family status and realized perhaps God *was* asking us to turn the looking glass of life on its head. Rather than take a passive position and wait for the nameless, faceless children to come to us, the joy set before us included taking a leap of faith and choosing to step out and go to them.

Through the power of the Spirit, an indescribable peace rested in our unified hearts. Together, we committed to take one step at a time and trusted the Lord would open or close doors according to His sovereign providence. The familiar feel of our family train was about to transfer to a different track. As the Lord aligned our hearts in this manner, for His purposes, Scott and I started to process the very practical implications of such a decision. We thought of almost nothing else. Our weekly lunch date conversations spiraled into single-focused discussions around this call. We balanced on the precipice of this leap of faith, but the question of how this would impact our current lifestyle constantly bubbled up to the surface.

We agreed I would make the permanent move to be a full-time stay at home mom. The Lord had already gone before us and prompted me to quit my job, so we were in sync there. But — another baby? Like, of the crawling variety? Lord, have mercy! The baby stages were hard enough for me the first couple of times. In fact, while in the throes of the baby blues after our second child, Brynn was born, I looked Scott straight in the eyes, grabbed him by the collar and declared, "If I *ever* tell you I want another baby, just say no!" He gladly obliged. Like-minded, we stacked hands on that one. No more diapers.

A pre-school aged child, three or four-years-old; now, that seemed more reasonable. (I'm sure those of you with preschoolers are aghast right now. The word "reasonable" is nowhere near synonymous with the word "preschooler"!) While I whole-heartedly agree with you, we wanted to keep our original birth order if at all possible, so that age range seemed to fit.

A boy or a girl? We had one of each, so we'd be open to either. Great. Domestic or international? We had a passion for the international community and Young Life (our life and vocational ministry involvement for the last 20 years) was flourishing in Ethiopia, not to mention the prevalence of adoptive families with Ethiopian children forming around us. God confirmed an "openness" to this country set in the horn of Africa, so we walked down that road.

We were, quite possibly, well on our way to having three kids. *What in the w*orld?! I know some people could raise three kids in their sleep while managing two full-time careers and hunting season on the side, but not us. No, this felt like a big deal. Man-to-man defense suited our natural parenting DNA more than the zone approach. Scott and Megan — two conventional characters, comfortable and happy raising two natural born children — were about to adopt one more. Or so we thought.

A couple of months into the paperwork, fingerprint and interview marathon that is the "home-study," Scott attended a work retreat at Young Life's Trail West Lodge; a beautiful family camp nestled at the base of majestic Mt. Princeton. As it turns out this would be the precise location of our next encounter with the whisper of God. When Scott returned, I knew something was up. He greeted me with the usual kiss, but quickly went off script. He didn't breeze off to dump his bags and change into more comfortable clothes. No, this time he lingered.

"What's up?" I teased as I sliced and diced bell peppers for that night's dinner.

"Well...I, uh, actually... I have something to tell you," he confessed.

"Wow, so serious!" My furrowed brow mimicked his.

"Okay, I don't really want to say this out loud, but I know I'm supposed to..."

I slowly looked up from my busy work and rested the knife on the counter. It was his turn to unload on me.

"The whole drive home, I listened to worship music and prayed about this decision. Every time I envisioned our future family, God showed me four children altogether. Not just three. I think we are supposed to adopt *two* children." His rapid speech surprised even him.

Ironically, some time back, I briefly entertained the notion of adopting a sibling set, but quickly dismissed the idea thinking it crazy because I knew full well Scott would never go for it and I wasn't exactly sure I could even handle four children. However, God revealed another plan in a way we knew it could *only* have come from Him. Another twist on this crazy journey.

After a long, deep breath in front of the computer, I emailed our international adoption agency and notified them of our shift in thinking. The keyboard seemed to have a mind of its own as I wrote that we might, maybe, possibly be open to adopting a sibling set if they were between the ages of two and six. Within minutes, my inbox lit up with a reply from our adoption coordinator:

"I will notify the main office, but I wanted you to know that your preferences fit just about all of our waiting children. If you want to see any or all of their files, let me know."

Whoa. That was fast. What could it hurt to just take a peek at a couple of pictures? No harm no foul, right? Almost immediately, photos filled my email inbox and penetrated my mind. Pictures of sibling sets and single children — all waiting to be adopted. Each face so sweet, but so unknown. I sat completely overwhelmed. These were photos of real kids, with real names and real faces. How would we, *how could we* ever decide?

"God, this seems impossible," I cried.

However, even as the pictures came, one photo in particular seemed to pop right off the screen. A young boy, no older than about six or seven stood a couple heads taller than his pint-size sister. He smiled brightly at the camera, exuding a bold heart and what seemed like a tender spirit. He gently reached for his sister's hand. Draped in a gauzy white dress, head shaved, she gazed up at him with adoring eyes. She was so tiny! How could she possibly be almost four years old as the profile claimed?

There was no logical explanation for the draw we felt towards these two, but it was undeniable. Once again, we invited Reese and Brynn into the discussion because we were a team. As the four of us stared at that grainy picture, we couldn't help but believe these two could potentially be *our* kids. There was just something about them.

Though the Spirit undoubtedly drew our hearts to these children, I still couldn't believe all this was actually happening. How could we possibly make an informed decision with only a photo and limited blood test results? I sat in bed each night that week and poured over several profiles. Maybe we'd heard wrong. Maybe we should back off and adopt just one child. After all, there were such beautiful boys available for adoption, too! I'm fairly certain if the intensity of my stare could have lit a spark, all the pages would have ignited into flames right then and there. However, at every pass, my eyes drew back to this sibling set. What was it about these two?

Once again, I scanned the profile page I had read and reread a hundred times, each time hoping I might uncover even one more ounce of information. His favorite color was still green, her favorite food, *injera*. According to the agency, they also had an older brother and sister in Ethiopia who apparently weren't up for adoption. I wondered what story simmered behind their eyes. As my intense stare practically bore a hole in the photo, my heart quickened when I noticed a detail I hadn't noticed before.

My gaze darted back and forth between the intake photo of the kids standing alongside their biological mother and the date at the top of the page. For all intents and purposes, the last moments they would ever see her sat captured right there on film. All three looked dusty and sad, dressed in ragged clothes, dark eyes rimmed with grief. The general look of trepidation on their faces was palpable. That's when I saw it...the date in the upper right corner of the page. The date the photos were taken.

This mother relinquished her children for adoption on *August 23rd* of that year due to extreme poverty and a terminal illness. Two injustices of the cruelest kind. I snatched my journal and frantically fanned through the pages. There, in my own handwritten scrawl, I re-read my groans of petition for the Lord to reveal His heart to us regarding adoption. The day I holed up at my kitchen table to fast and pray about this journey was that very day: *August 23rd*.

From that point forward, we tentatively shared our decision to adopt with family and friends. As expected, we received as many varied responses as there were people with whom we shared them. Some were excited and praised God in expectation of what He might do. Others were naturally fearful and protective of us. Shock coupled with surprise captured the general vibe. After all, our biological children were now ten and seven. We had been a strong team of four for many comfortable years. There are a myriad of ways to help children in this world, some purported. Why this? So permanent and unpredictable. What would this "do" to Reese and Brynn? Would they feel slighted, having to compete for our time and affection?

The emphatic responses were understandable. I could hardly blame folks for evaluating our decision because I had experienced these same reactions myself. Honestly, I didn't have a clear response to their questions. In fact, the more discussion that came my way, the more I wavered in my resolve. Maybe they were right, I speculated. Maybe there was another path. A safer path. However, no matter how hard we tried to grasp unanswerable perplexities we always came to the same conclusion. We could continue along our comfortable path, under the misguided perception that we had everything under control. That was certainly an option. However, in our heart of hearts we knew God was calling us to experience a new thing. In order to blow the top off of this life we had known, in order to move from *ordinary* to *extraordinary* we would have to trust and jump; two actions that do not come easily for a couple of type-A, organized, in-the-box planners like ourselves.

Can we really afford this, we wondered? Adoption is expensive and raising children sure ain't cheap. God replied, *"Do you trust Me?"*

"But, we're already serving you through our church and vocational ministry; isn't that enough?"

"Yes, dears, that's wonderful." Every human rebuttal to this God-given offer received the same retort from the Lord, *"That's nice..."*

No matter what we decided to do, we knew God would still love us. In fact, He might even still use us to advance His Kingdom. However, if we really wanted to experience more of Him, we realized it was ultimately up to us. Did we want "nice" or did we want "more?" God was clearly offering us a key to His kingdom; an invitation to experience Him in a brand new way. The question remained: Would we take it?

To follow God in this way seemed as mysterious as staring into a box of chocolates. The choices were overwhelming. Where does one begin? What would we uncover? What if we chose unwisely and came upon the taste of tangy orange marmalade instead of the sweet, sultry caramel we hoped for?

Come what may, we always reasoned we could manage biological parenting. That somehow that kind of parenting was in our natural wheelhouse. We could dig into the archives of the familiar and navigate this road with some (albeit false) sense of security. But God...Oh, that God! The thing for which we couldn't plan. The thing for which we couldn't prepare had implanted His heart in each of us. The world of the fatherless didn't need to be dropped on our doorstep. It had already existed for generations. We could wait no longer.

With that revelation, we prayerfully opened the metaphorical box of chocolates and stepped headlong into the adoption process. In some sense, I'm glad we couldn't see the inside of these treats before taking a leap of faith. Had I been privy to the reality that awaited us, we may have erroneously dismissed this unpredictable adventure for the comfort of the known. And you know what? We would have missed out. Big time.

However, I must confess, that first bite was anything but delectable. This invitation carried with it the very stark reality that we would need to dig deeper and love wider than we ever had before, and so would all four of our children. The Lord had given us a key to the Kingdom all right, but I began to wonder: Had we opened God's box or Pandora's?

Chapter 4:

Lost in Translation

"What you see and what you hear depends a great deal on where you are standing. It also depends on what sort of person you are."

—*CS Lewis,* The Magician's Nephew

To say I was a jumbled bundle of nerves the day we first met our Ethiopian children at the care center they called home for over a year would be an understatement of gargantuan proportions. The exhausting trek across the globe, feigning sleep on airport floors and nuzzling in with perfectly pungent strangers on a transatlantic flight didn't exactly help. Bleary-eyed and fueled by excessively strong Ethiopian coffee and adrenaline alone, we eked our way through Addis airport customs. While Scott stood in line for Ethiopian Birr and frantically calculated exchange rates, I scanned the environment, trying to glean any information I could about the social mores of this unfamiliar country.

In one corner, I noticed a woman clad in a beautiful, white cotton dress perched on a tiny wooden stool, bent over an open flame — yes, inside the airport! She steeped what appeared to be thick coffee and graciously poured it into petite ceramic cups, offering drinks to interested onlookers along with handfuls of popcorn. On the TV screen mounted on a nearby wall, another attractive woman strutted to the sound of Ethiopian jazz in what I could only presume was a well-loved music video. She wore a long, flowing frock and smiled atop a grassy mountain landscape. The woman threw her head from side to side and swayed in customary Ethiopian dance while brass horns blared a jazzy beat. It seemed safe to assume musicians and dancers like these were highly revered in Ethiopian pop-culture. The smell of incense filled the air.

We managed to clear the plastic tubs full of care center donations past suspicious customs agents and joined in mass exodus toward the parking lot. My face relaxed when a slightly built, well-dressed young man flashed a million dollar smile and waved us over. Yitbarek would be our driver. With over-sized containers safely tucked in the back and nary a seatbelt in sight, we dropped into the well-worn, springs-have-long-since-sprung seats of his dusty blue van. We bumped our way through pot-holed streets swarming with people and animals of all shapes and sizes. I wondered just how a city of nearly four million inhabitants could function with less stoplights than I could count on one hand.

It became abundantly clear, however, that stoplight or no stoplight, the only thing one needs to navigate the streets of Addis Ababa is a working car horn. Anything more is gravy. Just shy of full bumper-car status, "the zipper" was in full effect as cars squeezed past each other, nearly clipping duct-taped side view mirrors at every pass. I breathed a sigh of relief when we finally arrived at our destination intact. What felt to me like a nondescript back alleyway actually housed the entrance to the humble hostel we would call home for the next few days.

Yitbarek threw the gear shift into park and the van lurched to a halt. As we stepped through the iron gate and into the concrete courtyard, we noticed three other American couples chatting away just inside the entrance. Several Ethiopian children squealed as they chased a rubber ball through the cramped registration area. The ethnically diverse party beamed with enthusiasm at our arrival.

"Welcome!" one confident looking blonde shouted as she caressed the face of the pudgy brown baby squirming on her hip.

"You must be Scott and Megan! We are just about to head down to the care center to see the kids. Why don't you freshen up and meet us down here in about half an hour? We are more than happy to wait for you!"

The natural way these words fell from her mouth seemed so...ordinary, so nonchalant, as if it was just another day in the life. My response felt measured as I crafted an equally warm response, hoping my excited smile didn't betray my anxious heart.

"Absolutely! We'll, uh, be right down." I glanced at Scott for confirmation. He nodded.

Our steps echoed in the open stairwell as we climbed to our fourth floor room. What in the world were we doing? Somehow I figured we would have at least a day to settle in, catch up on some much needed sleep, and perhaps order a couple of drinks to settle the nerves. But, thirty minutes upon arrival? That afforded me just enough time to brush, flush, and grab the camera.

If I was *this* nervous, how on earth must the children feel?

As I hurriedly twisted my hair into a plastic clip in a vain attempt to look somewhat presentable, I gazed at the bathroom ceiling and, to my immediate horror, noticed the beast of all African beasts. A mosquito! Although I had packed practically every drug known to man, I was *not* about to be laid out by what I was certain was a malaria carrying offender. No sir. Not on my watch.

How did that ghastly beast get up there in the first place? I scanned the room and noticed the small dormer window above the toilet cracked open. Who on God's green earth could be so irresponsible, I wondered? Didn't they know malaria could kill a person? Not wanting to expose my fear, I decided against the idea of dragging my loving husband into my certifiable insanity. I knew full well he would jokingly judge my ridiculous paranoia and the plans I concocted to go Annie Oakley on this thing.

There was just one problem. I couldn't reach the window on my own. I'm 5'4" on a good day, back straight, pelvis tucked and wearing heels. (I did manage to refrain from packing heels on this trip!) Though some would call me short, I prefer the word "petite." Nevertheless, it was clear I couldn't reach the window from my vantage point on the floor.

With no step ladder in sight, I figured the next best thing would be to stand on the toilet seat. I am nothing, if not resourceful! I closed the lid, planted one foot squarely in the middle of the seat and pushed up. At once, the thin plastic cover gave way in a loud *snap, crackle, pop* and my foot plunged into the toilet! Needless to say, Scott enjoyed a healthy belly laugh at my expense and one of the two pairs of pants I packed was now completely soaked.

Thank goodness my ever-prepared mother reminded me to grab some powdered laundry detergent before our trip for just such an occasion. I washed my pant leg, set it out to dry and threw myself into a spare pair of jeans. As Scott continued to chuckle, we inhaled once again and joined the others waiting in the van.

I'm not sure how to describe the moments that followed because, to me, they felt more like an out of body experience than a physical reality.

Scott and I happily crawled over the others to get to the back seat where it would be much easier to listen, observe and (hopefully) remain relatively unnoticed. The intimate chatter between the other adoptive parents felt somewhat reassuring. Clearly they didn't appear stressed about the trip. They laughed and cooed at bouncing babies on their laps. I deduced we were the newbies of the group and even a 24-hour lead time seemed enough to put their minds at ease. They all appeared to know the drill and pointed out local sites along the way. One woman with a long, mousy brown pony-tail tapped Yitbarek on the shoulder and asked him to please pull over so she could buy a bunch of bananas to take to the kids. I later came to realize these types of donations from adoptive parents were about the only fresh produce present in the care center diet. If we didn't bring fruit on our visits, the kids didn't have any.

As the van wound its way through the chaotic city streets before breaking free on the outskirts of town, the lot of us introduced ourselves one to another. Each couple stated their first names, where they were from and the names and ages of the child or children they were adopting like they were ordering food at a drive up window.

After the others kindly repeated introductions for our ben-efit, all eyes fell on us.

"I'm Megan," I smiled. "And — this is Scott."

"We are from Colorado," he chimed in. "We have two biological kids at home who are eight and ten and we are adopting Kelel and 'Sen-yet.' At least, that's how I think you pronounce her name. Do you know which ones they are?"

I searched the faces of the other parents to see if I could gain any insight from their immediate reactions. Did they grimace? Did they smile? Did they raise any eyebrows or exchange questionable glances? I couldn't tell. They all just nodded in agreement.

The same blonde who appeared to be the leader of the welcome committee thought for a moment.

"Kelel and Sen-yet? Now which two are they…? Oh, yes! I think I know who you're talking about. They are so sweet!"

Relief swept over me. I hoped she was right. It was weird to think these virtual strangers had already held hands and intimately interacted with our kids because they arrived a day or two before us. For all intents and purposes, the other adoptive parents knew them better than we did. And they all seemed so...calm. And excited. Were they really that confident in their own journeys or did anxiety lurk behind the veil of their hearts as well?

Right in the middle of that private thought, Yitbarek turned into the final, bumpy back alley. The buzz in the van escalated. "We're almost there!" they exclaimed in familiar recognition. "Quick! Hand us your camera so we can record your first moments together!" In casual fashion, like this was a daily routine, each couple filed out of the van and formed a kind of receiving line. The last to emerge, Scott and I locked eyes as if to say, *"This is it. It's now or never. Let's do this thing."*

My feet fell like lead onto the dusty road. My heart raced so fast I thought I might take off running for the hills if I didn't concentrate on just breathing. I focused each breath in an effort to channel my own sort of adoption Lamaze technique. A woman emerged and unlocked the heavy rod-iron gate. As it swung open, we stepped over a 12-inch concrete threshold and into a whole new world. I had experienced the emotional transformation of being childless one moment to holding a slippery, wailing, most beautiful flesh-of-my-flesh baby the next. However, grafting two young children into our family — born of my heart, not of my flesh — proved to be a very different birthing experience.

We entered the small courtyard surrounded on all sides by a concrete wall topped with menacing barbed wire. Yitbarek sounded the Pavlovian *beep, beep* of the horn and children poured out the front door of the modest building. One young boy made a bee-line for Scott. This time, it was my turn to laugh! I realized I wasn't the only one strung straight out with nerves as I saw Scott bend down to hug this exuberant little fellow. As you might imagine, the boy was more than a little shocked. He frantically shook his head and pointed behind him. His jabbing finger indicated that Kelel was just a step behind. He was not our son. Heaven help us — Scott had picked up the wrong kid!

The photographs snapped that day (by folks with just a few more active brain cells than ours) were priceless. Void of any common language with which to communicate, kisses and hugs had to suffice. Even now, as I linger over the very first photo taken of the four of us, I can clearly see the strain in Scott's tentative grin and the questions behind my wide eyes.

Though quiet and skinny as a rail, Kelel carried himself with an air of cool confidence. Senait (pronounced 'Sen-ite,' rhymes with "tonight" as it turned out), carefully coiffed and tastefully dressed, seemed a bit more unsure. She tentatively climbed into my arms and turned her head toward the crowd of onlookers. A coy smile escaped her lips. If first impressions led us to any initial assumptions about our children's personalities, we could not have been more wrong! While parts of that day showcased pieces of their true selves, only time and a long bridge of hard-earned trust would uncover a more genuine picture.

That day slipped by in a surreal haze. Older children bounced around us in unison shouts of "Mama" and "Dad;" though we quickly realized those were the names given to all *"Ferengi"* (foreign) parents that passed through the gate, no matter the proper pairing. Kelel beamed with pride as he showed off *his* new Mommy and Daddy. We spent the better part of the morning following our new tour guide around the care center.

Albeit of modest stature, the two-story, salmon-colored stucco building seemed clean enough and the nannies' kind smiles brought comfort to our souls. The main floor housed the baby nursery, a tiny school room, and a small kitchen in the back. To my relief, there was also a little toilet room. No sink, but still. There were two bedrooms upstairs, one for the boys and one for the girls, along with a decent-sized living room furnished with a dingy brown couch and a small TV. Kids sat in a circle on the floor in the living room for meals and the older kids watched TV or movies for quiet time while the little ones napped in the afternoon. The front, concrete courtyard functioned as the outdoor play place. Kids kicked balls and jumped rope amid two rows of laundry drying on the clothesline.

Kelel guided us through the hallways and proudly pointed to the bunk bed he shared with at least one or two other boys at any given time. The hot, stuffy baby room proved to be the epicenter of activity. Cribs and floor space teemed with squirrelly babies — three to a crib — sitting, rolling, sleeping, crying, feeding themselves bottles or crawling from one side of the room to the other. Flies landed willy nilly without regard for personal space, and neither human nor fly seemed to mind.

The books and crayons we brought for the kids to play with couldn't hold a candle to the intrigue of our iPhones. Apparently kids clamoring for more screen time is universal and it didn't take Kelel long to figure out the basics. With an expectant look in his eyes, he would slide his index finger along the palm of his hand in a motion that indicated he knew exactly how to operate his new found addiction. The lifespan of the bubble solution we brought was about 30 seconds as Senait decided to dump it on the ground before refilling the plastic bottle with dirty water from the spigot on the side of the building. Her brow furrowed in confusion when she couldn't make a bubble emerge from the plastic wand and quickly discarded the obviously defunct contraption.

It became abundantly clear that not a soul in the place spoke English save the other equally Amharic-challenged adoptive parents practicing sign language with their children. During the pre-adoption paperwork process, we were told by the adoption agency that the older kids had English lessons every morning. *Awesome!* we thought. *This will give us a definite leg up.* Not so much.

There was an English teacher all right, but it turned out her language skills were limited to the 26-letter alphabet and a few non-essential (even slightly creative!) vocabulary words that the children chanted in unison each day like, "Multiplication, division, subtraction and 'equalization.'" In her tight little school room, older children took turns with a teaching stick and pointed to letters taped around the perimeter of the wall as they signaled to their counterparts to follow along: "A–apple, B–boy, C – cat," and so on. (In fact, when our children finally did come home they shouted, "H–house!!" every time we would round the bend towards home after an outing. After countless attempts, we eventually taught them the word was really just "house." No H. Even then, they remained skeptical.)

Thank the sweet Lord for the presence of a lovely teenage girl who was so excited to be headed to her adoptive home in Miami that she spent every waking moment pouring over her tattered writing notebook and appointed herself the care center translator. With her help, we managed to kind of navigate our way through the day. As the bright sunlight stretched into long shadows, Yitbarek (our driver and only known English speaker) returned for the nightly pick up to take us back to the guest house. His familiar face was a welcome sight to our worn-out bodies and to the children who greeted him with massive high-fives and bear hugs.

The ride back to the guest house was distinctly quieter than the morning trek had been. The couples adopting babies could barely tear themselves away from their delicate bundles of love while those of us who spent the day with the older kids, functioning as human jungle gyms and counting to 20 for interminable hide and seek games, fell exhausted into the van.

When we finally crawled into bed that night, still shell shocked from the events of the day, Scott rolled towards me and, with a voice that carried into the darkness of the night, muttered, "So…they *really don't* speak English…."

True that, Sherlock.

We spent the better part of the next few days visiting Kelel and Senait at the care center, where we filled up the digital camera and tried to wrap our minds around the profound reality of the events unfolding before us like a movie trailer. We caught glimpses of how life might look in the foreseeable future, but couldn't wrap our minds around a full-length feature film with our names in it.

Prior to our visit, we asked our adoption agency if it would be possible to meet any known relatives while we were in Ethiopia. Our social worker said she would reach out and inquire. She would need to see if Kelel and Senait's birth mom would be open to the idea and even then, anything could happen and the meeting could fall through. Either way, it was up to us to make the necessary travel arrangements just in case it all worked out.

We were eager and decided to buy plane tickets to fly from Addis Ababa to Mekele, filled with hope and faith that such a reunion might be possible. Miraculously, all the pieces fell into place. The profound impact of that encounter grabbed hold of my heart in ways I have a hard time expressing, even now. However, on the first Mother's Day we celebrated as a family of six (five-months after our eventual homecoming), I wrote my children — her children — a letter in an attempt to describe that day:

Dear Kelel & Senait,

This is a letter I write to you hoping one day you'll read it and know part of your history. Know how our hearts are forever linked to your birth country and your birth family. Know just how deeply loved you are — both here and there.

Not long ago, the probability of meeting your mother was just that — a possibility. Daddy and I had hoped to meet her, but there were no promises. To our nervous delight, however, your first mommy agreed to meet us, but it would be necessary for us to travel north to your native Tigray province.

Stepping off the plane in the wide open space of rural Mekele was a welcome reprieve from the cacophony of sights, never-ending sounds and significant array of smells that had surrounded our senses in Addis Ababa. Our eyes opened to an entirely different view of your beautiful country. We breathed deep the fresh mountain air.

After we visited the care center you had called home for nine months, now filled with other waiting children, we crammed ourselves into Tshaye's little red hatchback. I laugh, remembering his reaction when he picked us up at the airport. The look on his face was priceless as his eyes darted between his humble car and our American-sized luggage. Somehow we squeezed it all in, but I definitely wondered why in the world I decided to pack that last pair of shoes. No doubt we carried more in those suitcases than the sum total of most Ethiopians' worldly possessions.

Tshaye (the adoption agency's director in the region) and Birhanu (the local social worker) guided us through dusty streets and eventually navigated us toward the outskirts of town. Once free of the confines of the city limits, my heart began to race.

"We're getting closer," Tshaye observed. "We will get out of the car and walk from here."

"The place we are headed is not the children's original home," Birhanu reported. "Their mother has moved to a new location. This is good for you. Access to the other place would be at least a two or three mile walk."

As we traipsed up the pastoral hill full of grazing sheep and bleating goats, I noticed a little band of boys begin to pool in our path.

"These boys must wonder what in the world we strange-looking white folks are doing; wandering around this remote territory," I joked.

With a sideways glance, Birhanu replied, "I think one of them is Kelel and Senait's brother."

My heart stopped. I looked down to see one young boy in particular right on my heels. I looked at him. He looked at me. I bent down to stare into his sweet face. I recognized him from the thumbnail-sized school photo you had proudly shown us at the care center in Addis.

"Welday?" I squeaked.

His eyes, round as saucers, confirmed I had just connected with the first member of your family. In great haste, I grabbed my digital camera to pull up a picture of you two.

"Look! Kelel..." I pointed to your face on the small screen.

My exuberance quickly turned to deep compassion as Welday's eyes brimmed with tears. My naiveté betrayed me. I did not realize until that moment just how profound this experience would be. It was clear he missed his baby brother and sister. I can only imagine the questions that ran through his head; wondering what on earth would become of his beloved siblings.

The lump in my throat swelled as we reached the top of the hill. Your mother emerged to greet us, along with your older sister and your mother's new companion, an elderly gentleman wrapped toga-style in white cloth. To me, he looked like a quintessential tribal elder. His weathered face seemed much older than his chronological years.

The intimate details of that afternoon remain etched in my memory forever. Your mother prattled on in Tigrinya. We only received bits and pieces of translation from our social workers, but it was clear this meeting would change our lives. She welcomed us into her humble home and we are richer for it.

Stories were shared. Pictures snapped. Hugs exchanged.

Rights of motherhood transferred from one to the other. The most insane thing of all was that the "other" was me! Our eyes locked and tears flowed. A spiritual exchange took place in our hearts. This mantle was now mine to carry; a privilege of the highest order.

The weight of that day replays in my mind every now and again. The previously nominal holiday of Mother's Day now carries more meaning than I can convey in my meager attempts to write this story.

She gave me an extension of her heart that day. And you have grafted into an extension of mine. Much like a fine wine, our family is rich, complicated and beautifully complex. Your resilience astounds me. The fact that you let me into your hearts at all is an honor of the highest magnitude.

I am forever grateful — forever changed — because of how I met your mother.

This meaningful day proved to be a distinct turning point in our journey. The impact of that hug, that connection, those pictures and those tears seared a kind of bravery in my soul that gave me the courage to move forward. They also sent me straight to bed when we arrived back at our local hotel, due to sheer emotional exhaustion. I am not typically a napper, but my body welcomed a long one that day.

After that axis-altering encounter, Scott and I spent a few more days touring the gorgeous Axum and Lalibella regions. The locations and wonders we explored delighted our souls and increased our love and respect for the lavish landscape and layered history of Ethiopia.

The respite found in those days brought much-needed spiritual and emotional refreshment. Before heading home to the United States, we returned to Addis one last time to lavish hugs and kisses on our children and to assure them of our — Lord-willing — speedy return. (Kelel now confesses he didn't understand a word and thought that was the last he would ever see of us.)

We didn't realize the interim period between one visit and the next was less of an unnecessary inconvenience and more like God's way of preparing us for what lay ahead in the pre-liminary months at home as a newly blended family of six.

Chapter 5:

Grief – a Four-Letter Word

"No one ever told me that grief felt so like fear."

– *CS Lewis*, A Grief Observed

In the nearly five-month span between our first visit (which served as the stamp of approval from the Ethiopian courts) and our second (which sealed the adoption through the US Embassy), my mind burned with anticipation. I refreshed my email account day and night as we waited for the green light from the US Embassy to arrange travel to go and pick up our children.

One morning I woke particularly early; the sun was still hidden by darkness of night. This was no ordinary day, however. November 17th was the day my cousin Scott and his wife Jill were scheduled for their embassy appointment as they finalized the adoption of their 10-month-old Ethiopian baby girl. As the Lord arranged it, their embassy appointment and Kelel and Senait's birth mother's final interview were scheduled for the exact same day. There was a chance their paths might cross. I could hardly believe the timing!

Before I emerged from the comfort of my bed covers, I couldn't resist picking up my phone to check email one more time at the slightest hope of *any* news from across the sea.

I held my breath. The screen lit up. One more email:

"Right now we are at the Embassy and your sweet birth mother is sitting behind me as I type. We have been praying all day for her. The driver came by to pick us up for our appointment. We got in the car and they said they had one more stop. We would be picking up a birth mother. We instantly knew it was her. She is beautiful beyond words. Looks just like her picture. My eyes got teary as she got into the car with us and sat next to me. We are still in awe. We said Kelel and Senait's names and she smiled. Our guide explained the 'cousin' relationship between our daughter and them and she smiled. We are waiting for her to go in for her interview. She seems very peaceful. Talk to you soon." — *Jill*

A prayer for peace answered in real time! I just wished that same peace would penetrate my own heart, which seemed to beat at an ever-accelerated rate as I stared down the tunnel of the upcoming transition. Who was I to be nervous? My goodness! If my mind swirled with a thousand questions, the children must have ten thousand more.

We had learned bits and pieces of their story throughout the sixteen-month adoption process, while contributing virtually nothing of our own. Their limited knowledge of us was relegated to mere snapshots of a new brother, sister, mother, father and an "H-house" they would soon call home. A vastly different and unknown future awaited them at the tender ages of five and seven.

In early November, word came down from the US Embassy. They were ready for us to return to Ethiopia to pick up our children. This time, Reese and Brynn joined us on the trip. We wanted to bring them along so they might get even the slightest taste of the world from which their brother and sister were coming. Not to mention we wanted to start the attachment process between all six of us right away.

Our five-day stay in Ethiopia was a virtual honeymoon. Reese and Brynn took the lengthy travel and foreign culture in stride. They were beyond excited to meet their new siblings! We stepped into the care center courtyard one last time. Kelel was all smiles as he hugged his buddies and kissed the nannies good-bye. He posed willingly for pictures. Senait seemed timid, but crawled straight into my lap as Yitbarek drove us from the orphanage to the guest house. Both kids carried nothing but the clothes on their backs.

Kelel and Senait eased into the confines of the same fourth-floor room Scott and I had inhabited just five months earlier. They emptied the suitcases full of brand new clothes in no time flat. The contents lay in the middle of the floor like a pile of autumn leaves begging to be thrown in the air. All four kids enjoyed endless hours of fun jumping on (what I considered to be) one of the world's hardest mattresses, stacking and destroying Lego formations, and batting balloons back and forth. Each time a balloon popped, Kelel and Senait doubled over in hysterical belly-laughs.

The main level, stucco-walled courtyard absorbed the shock of the well-worn rubber ball as Scott, the kids and the guest house staff turned it into an impromptu soccer field. Inside, Senait slid back and forth across the tile floor with her feet covered, for the first time ever, in little pink socks.

The bathroom turned out to be another source of sheer joy and curious exploration. With nary a modest bone in their bodies, Kelel and Senait stripped straight down to their chocolate-colored birthday suits and took running leaps into the shower. What felt like a measly trickle of water by American standards was a downright, first-class waterfall to the kids. They splashed and giggled in delight as they lathered soap in their hair and skipped in and out of the shower yelling, "Washy, washy! Washy, washy!" each time leaving a veritable river of water on the floor in their wake. I also believe it's quite possible the toilet suffered "flush fatigue" by the end of our stay, likely happy to bid us a fond farewell.

By 7:00 pm each night, we wondered if a shot of Benadryl would calm the hyper troops. As Scott and I searched the minuscule English-Tigrinya dictionary we managed to rustle up for any phrases that might resemble, "good-night," "go to bed," "please," and "thank you," Kelel caressed his very first toothbrush. The minty cool taste of toothpaste met his tongue and his eyes grew big. No sooner did he start the back and forth motion along his gums than he spit into the sink. He grimaced and dragged me into the bathroom. The spit stuck on the side of the sink was not white, but rather a dark reddish-brown. He stuck his finger inside his mouth, pointed to the source of the pain, and groaned. Right away, we knew this was blood. Darn it. Where did that come from? Likely from a molar that would need tending to once we got home.

Our final day in country marked a momentous occasion for our family when the US Embassy stamped our paperwork and handed us two children's passports. "Congratulations!" the stately man behind the counter said to our entire crew. "Do you have any questions?"

Realizing they probably couldn't help us with the deeper questions that lurked in our hearts, we smiled.

"No, I, uh — guess that's that, eh?" I laughed. "Thank you for your service."

As the six of us boarded the redeye that night from Addis to Frankfurt, the phrase *"home for the holidays"* no longer felt like a marketing tagline; it was going to be a reality. We would be home for Christmas. What a wonderful gift indeed! Facebook messages streamed in from all over. Everyone back home was excited to meet our new crew. I just didn't realize that, as eyelids drooped while the wheels of the Lufthansa jumbo jet lifted off the runway, we were effectively stepping through the looking glass and tumbling head first down the rabbit hole.

Senait's trusting frame rested in a sweet little pile on my lap, but Kelel's eyes refused to close. It was as if a wild animal had just been coaxed (against his better judgment) into a giant cage. His eyes darted every which way and his hands pushed mine away as I tried to buckle him in his seat. A lovely German flight attendant finally persuaded him to relent to FAA safety regulations, but his senses still hummed on high alert.

"You have *four* kids! Wow. How do you do it?" she asked in admiration.

"Ha! Yeah…" I looked up at her. "I'm not sure, actually. We just adopted the younger two yesterday."

Somewhat taken aback, her eyebrows shot up as the corners of her mouth transformed into a little grin. She handed me a blanket and ambled down the galley, unsure how to respond.

Thankfully, the TV located in the seat back in front of Kelel showcased a movie which acted as a temporary sedative. Reese dutifully demonstrated how to plug the headphones into the arm rest. Once Kelel realized he also had full control of the volume and channel selection, the remainder of the flight seemed palatable as his eyes stayed glued to the ever changing screen. Kelel's taut body finally lost its struggle against sleep around 3:00 a.m. He dozed off just before we touched down in Frankfurt an hour later.

Scott shuffled off the airplane laden with extraneous bags and a sleepy Senait on his shoulder. The rest of us followed along like sluggish ducks in a row. We had five hours to kill before catching the bustling 9:00 a.m. flight from Frankfurt to Chicago, which meant one step closer to home. The meticulous German airport felt stark and overly bright at that hour of the morning. It seemed ours were the only heels that clicked down the echoing hall. Kelel emphatically insisted he carry his own stuff. His tight grasp on my phone didn't show any sign of abating either.

On our way to the gate, we rounded the corner to find a mode of transportation every sizable airport usually employs; an escalator. As we approached the giant silver conveyor that promised to magically transport us from one level to the next, Kelel's eyes widened in delight. He bound ahead before we could utter a word of caution and planted one foot squarely on the first rising step. Unfortunately, the other foot didn't follow suit. It rested on the stationary tile floor. The initial look of excitement turned to dread as panic ensued. In a scene that could have been lifted from Will Farrell's Christmas classic *"Elf,"* we watched, dumfounded as Kelel's legs spread farther and farther apart. Luckily, Scott had at least one wit about him and jumped in for the rescue. He toppled headlong over the rest of us and reunited Kelel's legs on the same stair for equal footing.

We located a spot in which to settle our crew for the duration of the layover; near the bathroom and shoved into a corner so we could keep close tabs on our unpredictable new recruits. Senait sat criss-cross on the cold, hard floor and proceeded to strip every crayon we had in our possession of its protective paper layer with her teeth like a hamster. Luckily, Brynn engaged her for quite some time with sheets of white paper.

"Draw on these," she instructed like a proud big sister. Senait acquiesced and spent nearly the rest of the layover filling the blank pages with teeny tiny circles.

Meanwhile, Kelel's pace increased to a frenetic nature. He was not content to sit, so I offered to take the first shift touring the concourse in an effort to pass the time. No extra naps for us. The airport shops burst at the seams with sparkly ornaments on artificial trees, multiple glass versions of Kris Kringle holding a bag of toys, and sugary pastries that seemed free for the taking. And what would make a previously orphaned child believe otherwise? In Kelel's mind, he had graduated from pauper to prince in a matter of days. The items on the open shelves were laid out like an endless buffet.

Each time his sticky fingers attempted to stow a new-found goodie in his backpack, mine countered and grabbed the item right back. His face tightened in dismay and confusion as I returned each knick-knack to its proper place. I realized I would not get out of the store without a massive meltdown on my hands if I didn't buy him something, so I raised my index finger and shoved it in his face as if to say, "*One! One!* I will buy you *one* thing." After much weeping and gnashing of teeth, he reluctantly settled on one thing and chose the biggest sugar cookie the store had to offer. We escaped without breaking or stealing anything. All in all, a success, I surmised.

Kelel hastily unwrapped the glistening cookie and sunk his teeth into his brand new treasure. His nose crinkled in disgust. The sugary sweetness offended his Ethiopian taste buds. He shoved the cookie at me with a look that dripped of blatant accusation.

"How could you let me pick that?" his eyes flashed.

I didn't need to plead my case, however, because just across the way, the duty-free shop caught his eye. He sprinted across the hall and ducked inside. By the time I caught up with him, the kid smelled like a bridal bouquet. My nose caught the scent of at least 25 different types of perfume. He navigated the aisles and casually sprayed each tester in the air before darting off to the moving walkway.

At that point, it was a game of cat and mouse. I was the cat, and he was the mouse. Each time I stepped closer and called his name, he cackled and sped down the walkway. Scott caught a glimpse of our shenanigans from his spot in the distance. I waved my hands above my head in a massive "SOS." Triage was in order if we intended to get on a plane with all four of our kids. He left the other three to fend for themselves and stood guard on one end of the moving walkway. I took my post at the other. Eventually, Kelel tired of taunting us and slid into Scott's man-sized grip. Crisis averted...for now.

We survived the connection from Frankfurt to Chicago by letting Kelel play on my phone. He bounced from colorfully stimulating app to colorfully stimulating app before he finally landed on the camera setting — one he could understand.

Nearly 24 hours (and 500 digital pictures and videos) later, we touched down in frosty Colorado Springs. Fresh fallen snow greeted our wide-eyed Ethiopians. The kids shivered as they rolled their bags through the parking lot in this foreign, frozen tundra. We hopped in our SUV, cranked up the heat and headed for home.

Our friends and family honored our request for privacy at the airport, but they had lovingly invaded our home while we were away. Candlelit lanterns lined the driveway and a huge butcher-paper banner hung over our fireplace that read, "Welcome home, Team Nilsen!" The fridge was stocked with chicken and eggs and the fruit bowl filled to overflowing on the counter. Our friends had prepared the way and I was oh so thankful! However, this Norman Rockwell scene didn't match the anxiety that welled up in my heart.

We were now home. No more translators. No more familiar sights and sounds. The kids were in shock. To look forward felt daunting and overwhelming, to say the least. Remember the tooth — the one causing all the problems? Yeah, it was on fire. We noticed the pain seemed almost unbearable for Kelel and it needed to come out. First order of business — call the dentist. They scheduled him first thing the next morning.

In an effort to provide me with some much needed sanity, Scott took Kelel and Senait to the appointment so I could recapture a bit of the old routine and take Reese and Brynn to school. With fresh wind in my sails, I shuttled the older two off to school and decided to hit the gym. Nothing a little elliptical cardio and a morning talk show couldn't cure.

Right about the time Kelly Ripa launched into her witty banter with some guest co-host and my elevated heart rate signaled I had burned a calorie or two, a text came through. It was Scott.

"Sorry to bother you, hon. I know you're exercising, but I need your help."

My heart sank, bummed to cut my workout short. I took a deep breath and dialed his number.

"Hey babe, what's up?"

In a matter of two hours, all hell had broken loose. While Senait couldn't get enough of being the center of attention in the dentist's office, Kelel flipped out. He wouldn't step within six-feet of the chair, let alone allow the dentist access to his mouth.

"I'm sorry," he told Scott. "I'm going to refer you to a pediatric oral surgeon. This tooth is about to blow. It must be extracted and he's going to need to be put under anesthesia to do so."

How on earth would we explain to this petrified child what was about to happen?

There was only one solution. We headed to our local Ethiopian restaurant to see if the lovely, Tigrinya-speaking owner could explain everything. Kelel's frenetic pace settled down while he enjoyed a piping hot plate of *injera* and *doro wat*. Through translation, we learned that poor Kelel was terrified because he presumed the dentist was going to take out *all* his teeth! Gracious, that would send me over the edge, too.

The next few hours scrolled by in a blur. We decided to divide and conquer. Scott took Kelel back to the dentist while I wrangled Senait for the afternoon. I managed to pick up Reese and Brynn from school, my mind not far from what was surely going down in the dental office.

As the two eldest sat focused on homework, I wiped the kitchen counter of after school snack crumbs, wondering what on earth was taking so long. The phone rang.

"Hello?" I answered instantaneously.

"Hey, hon," Scott managed over the intense moaning in the background.

"How'd it go?"

"Well, the tooth is gone. That's good. They said it looked pretty bad. But the doctor gave him a deep dose of anesthesia to make sure he was knocked out quickly. Coming out of it is *brutal*. I'm headed home. I can't talk. I have to hold him in the car with one hand and drive with the other. He is so disoriented. He wants to bolt. See you soon." He hung up.

Thirty minutes later, Scott entered the house carrying a 50-pound boy wailing in protest. A mixture of tears, drool and blood pooled into a wet circle that covered Scott's shoulder as Kelel fell onto the couch. His desperate eyes stared into mine before they trailed to something else behind me. Reese emerged from his bedroom, dressed to the nines in black slacks and a white button-down shirt. It was the night of the fifth grade band concert.

No sooner did Scott catch a glimpse of his handsome young son than he burst into his own chorus of tears. The vast disparity of the moment hit him like a ton of bricks. While he unsuccessfully tried to comfort one son who was disoriented and confused, he saw a picture of the other standing composed and ready to perform. Would life ever return to normal? It seemed impossible either of us could do the only thing we really felt like doing that night—attend Reese's band concert.

Scott, Kelel and I sat trapped in our grief. We all felt stuck and feared this tension, or at least some degree of it, would fill the sum total of the rest of our days.

Just then, the door bell rang. Our good friend Monet stood on the front porch.

"Hey guys — I just wanted to pop in and see if I could help in any way?"

One look at this sorry mess was all it took.

"Have you eaten anything?" she asked.

We shook our heads.

"Okay. I'm calling Jim. I'll have him bring over a couple pizzas."

Our shoulders relaxed. We nodded. We could at least take care of our immediate needs.

The Martins descended on our house to feed us and move us through the routine. I was thankful for the company and felt undergirded by their support and generosity. We encouraged Scott to head straight to that band concert. We assured him we would be fine and he needed to go. His reluctance quickly turned to relief. He changed into a clean shirt and headed out the door.

The first month together can only be described as intensely, extraordinarily other-worldly. Jet lag, communication barriers, and raw grief defined our days — and our nights. Understandably, Kelel was scared and unsure of his new surroundings. As such, he lashed out at anyone who threatened to breach his hard-fought autonomy. The biggest offender, in his mind, was me. He had a mom who loved him. Even though she wasn't able to care for him, she was still his mom and he did not like the idea that I might somehow replace her. No wonder he functioned scared and confused. One day he was living in *his* country with *his* people and the next, he was transported to a land where no one looked like him, spoke like him, smelled like him or acted like him. I'm certain I would have wanted to head for the hills, too.

One night in particular, I crawled into bed for some snuggle time with my then eight-year-old daughter, Brynn. Finally — the others were asleep and I could take a moment to exhale. As silent tears rolled down my cheeks, Brynn tenderly rubbed my arm. Under the cover of night, I pulled out my phone and emailed our social worker.

"What are we supposed to do?" I typed. *"How do we begin to create any semblance of normalcy when we seem to have lost all control? We need your help."*

I couldn't believe it had come to this. I was the mom, for heaven's sake! The one who's supposed to comfort my sweet little ones and tell them everything will be okay, not the other way around. I said as much to my dear daughter and she replied, "Well, Mom — you're the one that needs to be comforted right now. It's all going to be okay...isn't it?"

I rolled towards her and whispered, "Yes, baby doll. It will."

"Don't worry," came our social worker's quick response. *"We can help."*

A house call — and potential lifeline — was on the books.

Chapter 6:

An Inconvenient Truth – We Are Both

*"One of the greatest barriers to connection is the cultural importance we place on 'going it alone.' Somehow we've come to equate success with not needing anyone. Many of us are willing to extend a helping hand, but we're very reluctant to reach out for help when we need it ourselves. It's as if we've divided the world into 'those who offer help' and 'those who need help.' The truth is that **we are both**."*

– Brené Brown, The Gifts of Imperfection: Let Go of Who You Think You're Supposed to Be and Embrace Who You Are

I don't like to admit failure and I don't like to ask for help, but I especially don't like to ask for help when I feel like I've failed at something I chose to do. It's like somehow risking and failing is a shameful act, when I know in my heart that to risk and fail is better than to not have risked at all. Trial and error are also a very necessary part of life — especially if you want to grow or invent or produce anything of value. If any of my children said they wanted to run for student council against the most popular kid in school even though they might lose, I would tell them to go for it anyway. Of course! Because you never know, you might win. If you lose — well, hey — you tried and that will only strengthen your character. I would likely advocate for taking a risk even, and especially, if they are going to need my help and emotional support in the event of a loss. However, when it comes to my own decisions, I find it hard to let anyone in to help if the going gets tough.

God invited us to be part of a bigger story and we said, "Yes!" How could we now expect others to carry the burden we felt was ours to bear? Perhaps you have no frame of reference for this because you haven't believed the lie that it's better to go it alone, but if my hunch is correct, more than a few of you can relate. This kind of attitude runs deep in our Western culture.

Our family had reached a place where it was clear that we couldn't, in any way whatsoever, muster enough will power or do-it-yourself to overcome the struggle waging war in our home. I felt like I had failed all members of the family. There were at least two or more children at any given point who wanted to run away from home and, frankly, I wouldn't have minded doing the same. I was no longer the loving wife and mother I had tried so hard to become. We were desperate for help.

A few days after I sent the white-flag email, I opened the front door and saw our social worker *and* the director of the local adoption agency standing on our doorstep. They appeared like angels to me. My heart skipped with hope for some real time advice from tried and true experts; women who had walked this path with their own families and countless others.

"Welcome!" I chirped, perhaps a little too intensely. "Come on in…"

"Kids, come on into the living room! I'd love for you to meet a couple friends," I called.

Reese and Brynn responded quickly and extended their hands. Senait laughed and twirled around the room, clearly loving the spontaneous attention. Kelel's face tightened. He ran straight upstairs to our bathroom and insisted on taking a shower. I didn't know how to talk him out of it and I certainly didn't want to start World War III given the fact our social workers were seated within ear shot, so I reluctantly obliged the request. After what seemed like an eternity, he came downstairs smelling of extra soap, hair dripping with product. My sheepish grin served as a weak apology to the lovely ladies waiting there to help us.

For the next two hours, these dear women sat with us. They observed, listened, encouraged and ultimately gifted us with some much-needed tools for our parenting toolbox. Some of their ideas were familiar instruments in our hands — basic parenting practices we just needed to dust off and implement again. Others were more adoption specific. In some respects, we felt like first-time parents as we learned to wield those tools in our novice hands. These patient ladies reminded us our children had undergone tremendous change laden with layers of trauma. Their natural instinct was to buck the foreign system, much like a fever fights an illness. Their bodies and souls were not accustomed to this new way of life, so they did the only thing they knew to do — fight back.

As I tried to better understand this concept, the story of our patriarch, Jacob, came to mind and resonated with my tender heart. In Genesis 32 we find the account of Jacob wrestling with God. We don't know for sure why God chose to meet Jacob in that way, but ultimately, Jacob limped away with a more humble attitude and a permanent reminder of his struggle. After that encounter, God changed his name to "Israel" — which means "struggles (or, wrestles) with God." That was me! That was us. With every fiber of our fleshly beings, we wrestled with God and with each other in an attempt to resurrect the life we had just left behind. It wasn't the change that scared us, it was the loss. What is it about human nature that compels us to wrestle with the One who loves us most?

Just like Jacob wrestled, I wrestled. I resisted the will of the One who died for my sins; the One who wanted to lavish love and abundant blessing — not heartache and misfortune. Unfortunately, my half-empty perspective limited my ability to fully live into this love. Our youngest children operated in much the same way. As our social worker aptly conveyed, they were fighting for their lives. Our home was the third place they had lived in a relatively short period of time and they weren't sure they could trust us yet — maybe with their breakfast, but not with their future.

Even though *we* knew they had landed in a safe, loving (albeit human) environment, Kelel and Senait did not. They weren't ready to sit at the dinner table with us, let alone do life together as a family. They gingerly wet their toes in the safety of the shallow end and kept a safe distance of head and heart. Just as God beckons us into the vast adventure on the other side of the pool of life, we beckoned them to take our hands and trust our love.

The only difference — admittedly an *enormous*, game-changing one at that — is that *we* are human and *God* is divine. His love is perfect; our love is only made perfect through Him. His love remains unconditionally constant, while ours seems to vary depending on the hours (or lack of hours) of sleep we logged the night before or how hungry or irritated we are. Little did I know, in the vast darkness of those preliminary months, that God was actually preparing to do an even greater work with some tools of His own in, of all people, me!

Ever so gently, His firm hand lifted my head and invited me to begin the gritty, time-consuming task of sifting through the personal and corporate layers of grief. Undetectable with the naked eye, the parched roots of each member of our family desperately sought aquifers of water — water that would eventually lead us to the overflowing well of abundant life. This well hosts the Living Water of Jesus Christ, the water for which our hearts were truly thirsty.

Recognizing, naming, and owning our common thirst gave the Holy Spirit permission to enter and breathe life into our dry bones. God laid us on the loom of life and began to weave six individual threads into one colorful tapestry. Sometime in the months that followed, I listened to a sermon in which a pastor addressed his congregation regarding challenges they might face on their faith journey. He said, *"If you encounter resistance, there's most likely gold in them there hills!"* Boy, did we encounter resistance. It turns out, in order to mine the gold, I had to start by tilling a more personal soil — the soil of my *own* heart.

Honestly, until that point, I thought I pretty much had it all together. I was a capable, loving wife and mother. I had experienced fulfillment (after serious trial and error) in the work world and had chosen to stay home with my kids as a matter of personal calling. Friends could lean on me. Sisters could cry on my shoulder. Just say the word and I would be there. The moment our children came home, however, my world — along with theirs — turned completely upside down. I was no longer the calm, cool and collected individual I fancied myself. I had no inspiration or wherewithal to figure out what to eat, let alone how to go about the multi-step process of putting a full meal together. I barely found time for a shower!

Nearly every time Scott left for work in the morning, our world turned inside out and the atmosphere on the home front spiraled out of control. A battle of wills over just about anything could turn into a three-hour standoff or worse. Invariably, Reese would come running and silently mouth, *"Do you want me to call Dad?"*

"Yes!" came my emphatic reply.

No sooner did Scott greet his co-workers, set down his coffee and open his email than he would pack everything back up and head home like a first responder racing to the scene of an emergency. I felt — and looked — like the walking dead and everyone knew it. Everyone knew it and they came to support us. Friends, family and people we hardly knew took time out of their lives to help take care of us. At least from what I could tell, people suspended any pre-conceived judgments. No matter what people thought or uttered behind closed doors about our family and the reality of the choice we had made, we felt nothing but love from our tight-knit tribe. There are no words deep enough or wide enough to accurately describe the buoy our community was to us in those dark hours.

Meal sign-ups increased in proportion to our desperation. My phone and email lit up with words from folks praying for us, interceding for us and even fasting on our behalf. I still get a little choked up when I recall the vast array of support we received. However, despite the tremendous outpouring from so many, I still couldn't shake a type of sadness that simmered like a constant low-grade fever. I wasn't so sick with depression that I couldn't get out of bed, yet I wasn't my normal, happy-go-lucky self either. Tears threatened to breach the carefully constructed barrier at any moment. It was tough to make eye contact when people asked how I was doing and Facebook was not a place I wanted to visit.

Social media portrayed everyone else moving about their lives with joy and ease. Friends begged me to post pictures of our first weeks together, but I couldn't bring myself to do it. Posting photos of happy, smiling faces felt deceptively incongruent with the private reality that raged inside our home. I longed for a sense of balance, or at least a sense that I wouldn't always be operating on the verge of a nervous breakdown.

God led us into this journey, of that we were certain. We recognized the invitation to go deeper with Him and we answered the call. But what does one do when the reality of answering the call feels too big, too heavy, and too sad to endure for any length of time? The euphoria of following Jesus all those many months prior melted into confusion and despair as days and nights held broken pieces of shattered lives.

The counter-culture Beatitudes Jesus preached in His famous Sermon on the Mount in Matthew chapter 5 never felt more alive to me. They seemed to leap off the page as I resonated with them in a new way. I was "poor in spirit," without breath to take another step. I realized my insatiable need for God and longed to experience the promise spoken by Jesus Himself. He said the Kingdom of Heaven would be given to such as these. An intimate encounter with this promised Kingdom is what prompted us to go on this journey in the first place. I wanted to experience that so badly, so why wasn't I seeing it?

Not to mention, we lived in a house full of people who mourned for a life we once knew and comfort seemed far from us. I was incapable of comforting the ones who depended on me the most. Nor did I sense my own blanket of comfort from the Lord. Scott and I often found ourselves "self-medicating" at night as we lay on the couch staring at the television. We inhaled episodes of anything that made us laugh or cry or promised to temporarily transport us from our current reality. That felt like comfort. At least, until it didn't.

For the first time in my life, I lay flat on my face before God. Sure, I had taken risks in the past, done things slightly out of my comfort zone, but each of those things had been for a time or a finite season. There had always been a light at the end of the tunnel, but I couldn't see the light this time. Would extreme grief define the sum total of the rest of our days?

I grieved for my newly adopted children, who had just lost everything and everyone they had ever known. They felt ripped away from the country they loved because, quite frankly, that was their reality. I grieved for my biological children, who watched the Mom and Dad they had always counted on, played with and cuddled with — the parents from whom they received all the attention in the world — fall apart before their very eyes (with no semblance of subtlety, I might add). All pretense flew out the window as grief loomed large over our home.

We couldn't communicate with one another and every interaction felt stressful. Kelel didn't understand English any better when we spoke slowly or loudly, nor did he comprehend that food on grocery store shelves wasn't his for the taking. On our first outing, he haphazardly threw meat tenderizer, Mother Mary Christmas cards, vanilla scented candles and Febreeze spray into the cart. I tried to put them back without him noticing. He noticed. Over budget and over tired, I left with the groceries I intended to buy and many I did not.

I continually mopped up soapy water over those first weeks at home, due to Senait's insistence on splashing in a warm bath several times a day. While chaos swirled within our walls, Reese withdrew into the shell of his own mind, finding video games to be a welcome reprieve. Brynn's eyes welled with tears whenever one of her new siblings mindlessly bopped her on the head and she wrapped a pillow over her ears each night to drown out the protests of her new siblings resisting the bedtime routine.

For quite a while, we drove in the car with kids unbuckled in their seats because the concerted effort it took to convince Kelel and Senait to click one metal end into the other resulted in Mommy losing a hard-fought battle every time. Only four of us made it out of the car and into the Christmas Eve church service that year. I sat in the back row of a packed sanctuary, flanked on either side by Reese and Brynn while Senait sat on my lap, sustained by a multi-colored candy cane. I could hardly focus on the babe in the manger, however, because my mind drifted to the two locked in a heated battle of wills in the car in the parking lot. "Silent" was not the word to describe that night.

I remember going out to lunch with another adoptive mom shortly before we brought our kids home. At that time, I wanted to glean *anything* I could from *anyone* I could in hopes of putting some framework around our journey. This particular mom adopted two boys from Ethiopia right as she and her husband were on the cusp of becoming empty-nesters. I noticed we had mutual friends on Facebook, so I sent her a message and asked if she would be free to mentor me for an hour or so over fish tacos and a Diet Coke. She kindly agreed.

No sooner did our bottoms hit the booth than I peppered her with questions. I soaked in each word that came from her mouth. The homecoming transition had been hard for them too, but not necessarily in the way one might expect. In their case, the adopted boys actually settled in quite well. Language proficiency grew exponentially and the boys had found lots of friends at school and success on the soccer field. The rub, she explained, was actually in her own heart. Though the transition period manifested differently in each member of their family, it was hardest for her personally.

After she shared her story, I light-heartedly joked, "All right! I hope you don't take offense, but in some strange way I feel relieved. If the hardest person to deal with in the wake of this whole transition is going to be me, well — I'm adept at dealing with that! I may not be able to control other people, but at this age I sure as heck better be able to get hold of myself." Little did I know how ironically prophetic that conversation would be.

Even though the transition for our family was less than smooth, the fact remained that I was the one spiraling ever downward. I knew I needed to find help — and fast. If not, I was in jeopardy of being no earthly good to anyone under our roof. I knew the Lord promised never to leave me nor forsake me, and I knew He would show up to comfort and guide, I just didn't know *how* or *where* to look for the fulfillment of these promises. How would I find the buried treasure when I couldn't see the forest for the trees?

I had been a Christian nearly my whole life and yet, in a time of trial, I began to sink. It was high time to shed any facade that conveyed I had it all together. Vulnerability would be the key to breakthrough. If I could lay my soul bare before the Lord, then He could come in and do the work only He can do. There was gold to be had, I just needed to agree to do the work it would take to discover it. Unearthing treasure takes loads of time, a dash of risk, a dollop of faith, and whole-hearted agreement to be led into the most vulnerable of places.

The words of King David in Psalm 34:17-19 became a lifeline for my soul, *"The LORD hears his people when they call to him for help. He rescues them from all their troubles. The LORD is close to the brokenhearted; he rescues those who are crushed in spirit. The righteous face many troubles, but the LORD rescues them from each and every one,"* (NLT). A new beginning waited just beyond the bend, though the tables had turned. No longer was I the one helping others; it was I who needed to ask for help. No longer was I the one counseling others with a sympathetic ear. I was the counselor that needed a counselor!

A quote by twenty-first century missionary, Frank Laubach painted a picture for me that exemplified this reality even more. He wrote, *"Somebody was telling me this week that nobody can make a violin speak the last depths of human longing until that soul has been made tender by some great anguish. I do not say it is the only way to the heart of God, but I must witness that it has opened an inner shrine for me which I never entered before."*

Great anguish had tenderized my tattered soul. I longed to be in unison with the heart of God, but the journey to get there required I shed any pretense and willingly visit an (as yet) untouched inner shrine. I desperately wanted to see the goodness of the Lord and take back my rightful place in the land of the living — for my husband, for my children, and for me. I picked up the phone and scheduled my first counseling appointment.

Chapter 7:

"Motherhood is Not Your Greatest Calling..."

"So you should not be like cowering, fearful slaves. You should behave instead like God's very own children, adopted into his family — calling him, 'Father dear Father.'"

—Romans 8:15 (NLT)

"**M**otherhood is not your greatest calling," Linda replied after I poured my heart out regarding the sheer gravity of our situation. I sat aghast. My mind twirled in circles as I tried to process these words spoken in love and disarming honesty by my therapist. (As a matter of semantics, I prefer to say "therapist" over "counselor." I believe one gets a better rate of return on the listener's reaction. Going to "counseling" implies your life needs a little tweak, the gentle hand of a dashing dance partner. "Therapy" conveys the idea that you need to be hit over the head with a 2' x 4' in order to avoid derailing this train, taking a nose dive, and dragging innocent bystanders down as collateral damage.)

In any case, at this point in my journey I didn't need the listening ear of a safe, easy-going confidante. I had those in spades. My friends, my sister, my family (God bless them every one!) were invaluable as they listened and cried with me. Rather, a more profound, locked away, private part of me needed someone who could cut to the core of the issue in a new way; someone who could shed light on some darker demons and steer me towards freedom. Whoa, Nelly, did I find that voice! It's just, at that particular moment, seated on that particular couch, those particular words cut straight to the bone.

My jaw dropped and my brow furrowed. What could she possibly mean by this offensive phrase? If motherhood was not my greatest calling, I could only assume my life was now a complete and utter fraud. I had dedicated my whole life to being a mom. Days and nights were no longer my own. They belonged to four people who, by all accounts, depended on me. Believe me when I say I'm not the kind of girl who always dreamed of becoming a mother. Sure, I imagined I'd have kids one day, but I also wanted a career. Throughout my childhood, I watched my very capable mother deftly juggle kids and career. I figured that's how I was wired, too. In fact, I previously enjoyed my part-time job as a school counselor so much I found it quite difficult to finally make the leap and commit to being a full-time, stay-at-home mother of two — let alone four!

In all honesty, Scott and I had entertained a heated discussion about this very issue the night before the appointment. Just before I drifted off to sleep that night, my mind whirled, ablaze with frustration. My body was tired. My heart ached. I wasn't sure I really wanted any part of this new life. It sounded ugly even when I said it to myself, but I couldn't hold it in any longer. I figured there was no time like the present to unload these feelings so I wouldn't have to carry them alone. Perhaps, in some twisted way, I wanted him to feel my pain too. Was this selfish? Yes. But isn't honesty always the best policy? Not necessarily. Regardless of any potential fall-out, I had to let him know how I was feeling.

As I hurled my pain, hoping some would stick to him and I might feel even the slightest bit lighter, he crafted a come-back of his own. Clearly, I cut to the core and wounded the one I loved the most. With eyes cast steadily at the wall, he offered a piece of his heart in return.

"I haven't been able to put in a full day's work in over two months..." I could tell he was just getting started.

"I spend all day, every day picking up shrapnel from everyone's emotional meltdowns," he continued. "I am doing everything in my power to keep this family from entirely imploding. I am making all the sacrifices I can and appar-ently it still isn't good enough. Babe, what more do you want from me?"

"Sacrifice..." I snarled. "You want to talk about *sacrifice*? My whole *life* is a sacrifice."

Then it happened. The words I could never get back.

"*Motherhood* is a sacrifice!"

The words hung in the air like a lead balloon. Pain and ugliness unleashed into the atmosphere. I thought getting my emotions off my chest would somehow make me feel better. It didn't. Speaking those words out loud actually made my stomach churn. How had I, a fun-loving, dedicated mother and Christ-follower, become such a self-absorbed, self-cen-tered, frustrated shell of a woman?

I recounted this very story to my therapist the next day, thinking I was bound to find a sympathetic soul! After all, she was a mother too. But no. Do you know what she did instead? She graded me. That's right — she gave me a *letter grade*. She told me my selfish, fleshly response to Scott amounted to nothing grander than a big fat C+. I had never, to that point, received that poor of a grade — especially regarding behavior. I worked hard to garner A's and B's in school. If hard work didn't pay off, I figured flattery could get me anywhere. However, in all my adult days, no one had ever called me out with such boldness.

I felt offended, and then — convicted.

I knew it wasn't right to unload on Scott the way I did, but in the name of all things vulnerable, authentic and honest, I really didn't see any other way. My back was against the wall and I felt stuck. All I really wanted was to enjoy my life, to relish my kids and to be a great wife to my husband. However, in all three areas I came up short.

At the inception of our adoption journey, many people asked me the same question when I told them we were adopting. After the slight shock and initial pleasantries, it wasn't all that uncommon to wade in a little further, "Do you think it is possible to love an adopted child just as much as a biological child?" they wondered. I didn't know the answer at the time, although I sure hoped it would be possible. At some level, I believed it could be possible. Why would God invite us into such a journey if it weren't? However, now after much reflection, I believe the answer is both "yes" and "no." Let me explain.

To a two-dimensional question like, "Do you think it's possible..." there can only be a two-dimensional answer. Both the question and the answer are limited by finite reality — a reality tethered to what we know of human love on this earth. Human love is, after all, human; confined by mortality and finite, concrete reality.

When my counselor declared motherhood was not my *greatest* calling, could she actually be proposing an alternate reality? A greater calling of a different kind? One in which I might truly be *in* this finite world, but not *of* it? Was it possible God's Holy Spirit could renew my mind in such a way as to transform my entire being? Even if my circumstances didn't change, would I be able to operate in a different realm? The mere hint of the promise of these truths felt like water to my weary soul. They provided hope. I knew my own strength had failed me and, by extension, everyone around me. That much was clear. My own strength was (and is) distinctly and utterly *human*.

In my own strength (that is to say without access to a supernatural reality), I am capable of loving a warm sunny day in the mountains, the fragrant smell of the lilac bush nestled outside my living room window, or a kindred soul who shares my passion for a good latte and an even better bargain.

In my own strength, I am capable of loving and even *liking* a child (biological or otherwise) who listens to and cheerfully obeys my every word, a husband who bends over backwards to give me much coveted free time and even folds the laundry while I'm gone, or a God whose perfectly laid plan falls in step with my own.

In my own strength, I am capable of loving and even *liking* myself on a day when I've taken the dog for a run, dusted the baseboards (like that *ever* happens), paid the bills, tickled my children and bandaged a skinned knee — on a day when my first reaction to an unruly child isn't one of frustration, but one of patience and tender loving care.

Man, I am all over that ... *in my own strength*.

In my own strength, I fall pitifully, unmercifully short of manifesting the kind of love it takes to really love the way Jesus loves any of my children. Or, on a grander scale, all of *His* children. To love with unabashed passion when none may be given in return. To love the naturally unlovable in both others and myself. To love with the kind of selflessness it takes to fully lay down your life for another. To love in such a way that I would truly believe *all* my children are God's and not mine; that they are His gift to me — no strings attached. None — no, not one — of these things can be fully accomplished in my natural strength.

That day on the therapy couch brought the revelation light of a new dawn. If I seek my primary identity solely in the mothering of my precious children, I may feel lifted up...for a while. However, we are human and kids grow up. However well intentioned, we are all broken.

Yes, I do love all my children "the same." But that "sameness" happens to be mortal and fallible. I would actually be *withholding* a certain amount of love from my kids if I only chose to love them in my own strength. If I prioritize anything or anyone above getting to know the penetrating, unconditional love of my Father God to the point where His Spirit flows through me on a continual basis, emptiness and disappointment will inevitably rear their ugly heads. I am learning my base identity must be found in Him alone. My primary identity must come from my relationship with Jesus. Because when I am in Jesus, when I spend time with Him, when I gain my identity *from Him – I am free*. If I can believe, embrace and ultimately live into the fact that I am a daughter of the King; well, that changes everything!

At that point, I am no longer bound to the confines of this world. I am free to love, to be loved, and to live loved. I am free to embrace the woman and mother He created me to be — for the ones woven in my womb and for the ones woven in that of another.

Motherhood is about *daughterhood*. It's about seeking to find my true identity in Jesus and modeling that — for my kids. My efficacy as a mother flows directly from my dependency on my Father. Only then am I free to fly the way God intended.

Indeed, motherhood is *not* my greatest calling — *daughterhood* is.

And fatherhood is *His*.

Once I truly opened my heart and mind to absorb this fundamental truth, everything shifted. I don't mean to imply circumstances changed overnight and everything came up rainbows and roses. Rather, my mind-set shifted. I realized I had confined my life (and my mothering) to a certain box, that somehow motherhood was more about *doing* than *being*. However, the adoption exposed the dark underbelly of this way of thinking. By His grace, the Lord helped me see it is really the other way around. Certainly, my to-do list remains a mile long and then some, but that list, those chores and tasks represented therein, do not define me. They are part of what I do, but they are not the sum total of who I am.

To be a mother means to provide, to nurture, to teach and to raise. To be a daughter means to receive, to be taken care of, to learn, and be led. There is a supernatural role reversal here, a sort of *beautiful exchange,* if you will. When I approach each day as a daughter of the King, I position myself in a posture of humble dependence and gratitude. In effect, I am ready to receive my assignment from my Daddy. When I open my mind to this way of thinking, I am more likely to be the unique version of the mother and woman He created me to be. The key to breakthrough is less emphasis on the task and more emphasis on the relationship.

This truth plays out in real time almost every day as I mother my children. God uses my relationship with them to remind me of this. When I snap my fingers, bark orders, or speak in motherly Morse code, my children bristle accordingly. However, when I take the time to breathe deep, sit down, look them in the eye and really *listen* to their hearts, the outcome is exponentially better. Heaven knows I'm nowhere near 100% on this one, but I'm learning. Baby steps.

When I focus more on the relationship than the task, I continue to build layers of trust. My children realize I care more about them than the requested obedience and they are 110% more likely to actually do what I ask because we've built another layer of trust. It goes full circle. Again, I'm no expert here, but a journey of this nature is way more likely to bring about the abundant life than when I rule with an iron hand.

Efficacy as a mother flows directly from my position as a daughter. Even though motherhood is a call of the highest magnitude, it is not, and *should* not, be the sole definer of who I am. When I can release my vice-grip on personal control (which is a counterfeit idea anyway) and learn to put God first, then I allow Him the space to be Father and I can be daughter. When I realize my good Father only wants the very best for me, I learn to trust His heart. For, *"which of you fathers, if a son asks for a fish, will give him a snake instead?"* (Luke 11:11). When I trust His heart, I approach my day eager to walk in obedience to Him.

Only after beginning to understand this pivotal, paramount truth could I start to write a brand new chapter. I walked away from my therapist's office that day a bit dazed and confused, but I clung to a profound new clarity I had never before understood. Even though I once peered through a mirror dimly, I had now effectively stepped through the looking glass. A bright new world waited on the other side. A light shone at the end of this tunnel; a light that has since revolutionized my life and radically enhanced my walk with the Lord.

I am not defined by the outcome; rather, I am molded by the process. When I find peace in the process — meaning, in the sovereignty of a righteous and loving God — that peace (and freedom) flows into the details of my life, both big and small. I am no longer slave to the enemy's lair of lies. Sure, Satan fires arrows from time to time, but my sensitivity to God's voice allows me to fight the battle in new and, honestly, more effective ways. I am slowly but surely learning to walk in freedom and truth, shedding long seeded remnants of control and fear. The challenge now remains not simply to *believe* it in my head, but to *live* it.

Just as James exhorts in chapter 1 verse 27, it is a beautiful extension and manifestation of our faith to *"care for orphans and widows in their troubles..."* However, my new-found clarity opened my eyes to the often neglected second part of that verse. James closes out this exhortation with a more insidious command, which is, *"to refuse to let the world corrupt us."* This is precisely what happened to me. I'm guessing the manifestation of this idea might look different for each one of us, but it soon became clear to me that I, for one, had let the world move in and take up residence in my heart.

What exactly did this worldly corruption look like? It was not pretty. I had begun to question the entire call. In the name of all things good and helpful and well-meaning, had we actually ruined two children's lives — not to mention our own? This perspective threatened to take us all down with no hope of coming back up. Not a place I wanted to be. Not a place God wanted us to be.

So, how was I supposed to get rid of this insidious problem? How would I uproot corruption's nasty hold and start planting a new way of thinking that would ultimately lead to the freedom and peace I have just described?

That, my friends, was the task at hand.

Chapter 8:

Corruption Ain't Just a River in Washington, D.C.

*"As for me, I never lived, I was half dead, I was a rotting tree, until I reached the place where I wholly, with utter honesty, resolved and then re-resolved that I would find God's will and I would do that will though every fibre in me said no, and I would win the battle **in my thoughts.**"*

— *Frank Laubach*, Practicing His Presence

Corruption is one hairy, audacious, beast of a word. Movies are made about it, journalistic exposés written on it, court cases drafted over it, scandals birthed by it. Some government systems are even built on it. However intriguing to read about, it's not a good thing in which to be involved. Or, so I've been told. The definition of "corrupt" includes words like, "bribery, lacking integrity, crooked, depraved, perverted, and wicked." If that doesn't paint a gruesome enough picture, try these words on for size: "infected, tainted, decayed, and putrid." Not really how I'd prefer to be described.

A girl like me would be best leaving such things well enough alone! No corruption for me today. I've got enough fish to fry explaining modified fractions to tearful children plodding through homework on a Tuesday afternoon, rogue socks to reunite with their mate, in-house squabbles to referee... Nope, involvement in a corruption scandal is not on my ever-increasing to-do list. I'll leave that foolishness to the uber-wealthy, ultra-entitled, morally depraved leaders of — really, just about anywhere! But me? No. I have plenty of other junk to deal with and corruption isn't one of them, thank you very much.

Or — is it?

As I pondered the highly publicized James 1:27 verse, the catalyst of many people's involvement in the orphan crisis (including our own), the Spirit began to highlight the second part of the verse. Frankly, I don't think I ever paid much attention to it up until now. So often I happily camped in the *"help the widows and orphans in their distress"* part, which is good, and necessary and a very real manifestation of God's heart! Please don't misunderstand me. I still believe engagement with orphans and widows and any marginalized population of society is absolutely one of the most profound ways to align with the heart of God. Nevertheless I, quite literally, glossed over the latter part of the exact verse that spurred us on our journey in the first place. For some reason, probably because they hit too close to home, those words took a back seat to the others.

James implores Christ followers to not only seek out *"pure religion,"* but we must also live *"above reproach."* As children of God, we are to *"refuse to let the world corrupt us."* When we allow the world's insidious grasp to take hold of our thoughts and actions, we no longer shine like stars in the universe. We look and act just like everyone expects us to act; subject to living under the influence of the world. We become perfect pawns in the enemy's schemes.

The original Greek word for "corrupt" is *aspilos,* which means "free from censure, irreproachable, unsullied." However great our works and deeds appear, they are but clanging gongs if they lack genuine love (1 Corinthians 13). The very works we do in the name of Jesus could likely drag us into a miry pit of religiosity if they aren't countered by a deep, humble hunger for righteousness. Psalm 23:3 reminds us that God *"leads us in paths of righteousness for His name's sake."* We hunger and thirst for more of Him so that He, not we, may become famous. We want to glorify Him in a sort of holy, divine circle.

This all sounds well and good on paper, but just how, pray tell, are we mere mortals, wretched people prone to wander, supposed to live spotless lives — unstained by the world's ways? James 3:6-8 tells us our tongues are the worst offenders of all and *"no man has ever demonstrated the ability to tame his [or her] own tongue!"* Heaven knows I'm still working on that one.

We were born into *this* world and we currently live in *this* world. It stands to reason our fleshly selves only know how to operate in a concrete, finite reality. Our physical bodies naturally orient to what the ancient Greeks called *chronos* time — that which is a specific and firmly set amount of time. Our physical lives represent this finite (*chronos*) timeline. The familiar cycle goes from birth to life to death, in that order. We all know what it feels like to get sick, run down, annoyed, and lose our temper. At least, I know I do! By nature of deductive reasoning you know, me being human and all, that I might conclude at least most of you know what it feels like to brood over the past and fret about the future to some degree. Furthermore, those nasty tongues often don't know when to call it quits.

The utter humanness of corruption and depravity of spirit blossomed and grew horns in my own heart when our children came home from Ethiopia. Each day I looked in the mirror and marveled at the hollow face staring back at me. What was I doing? Nothing in me made me fit to be Kelel and Senait's mother. Words failed us. Eyes averted contact. Even gentle hands were unwelcome to the touch. Senait fluttered and flitted about with nary a care in the world. It seems her relatively young age and go-with-the-flow personality protected her in those moments. However, sweet Kelel was another story. His grief came from a place so deep no human touch could provide comfort; least of all mine. I had built up such expectation that this new life, this new family would portray the most beautiful portrait of the Kingdom, but in those preliminary moments together, it felt like anything but.

My corrupt soul wanted to run, fast and hard, away from the hurt that swirled on all sides. I knew in my mind that I was born again — destined for a new, eternal, no-tears-in-heaven kind of life. I knew my salvation was a direct gift from the blood and sacrifice of the spotless, *uncorrupted*, unstained, untainted blood of the Lamb of God; but in the darkness of night, I couldn't help but wonder how that knowledge was supposed to help me in the present moment. I could concoct a whole host of scenarios in which the afterlife would be the most amazing, fulfilling, *Guinness Book of World Records* worthy, mind-blowing, God-honoring experiences where I (Lord willing) would be reunited with lost loved ones. But what about life on this side of the veil, the one we're all living right now?

How does dreaming about a future heaven help me rein in my emotions when any given pairing of my children bicker for the umpteenth time and my frustration level goes from 0–60 in .5 seconds? How does envisioning celestial cherubs dancing around motivate me to pick up a piece of broccoli when I have the munchies instead of a bag of chips? When the phone rings and life changes in an instant, when a marriage feels like it has flat run out of hope, when a child walks out the door and you wonder if he will ever return — what then? However true, waxing eloquent about the promise of heaven sometimes brings little solace to a soul struck by the deepest grief.

Author Emily P. Freeman suggests in her book, *A Million Little Ways*, that our "job [here and now] is to carry out the inner desire of Christ" and the "inner desire of Christ is to bring glory to the Father." If bringing glory to the Father is the litmus test for life, then by all accounts I was doing a pretty lousy job. I wasn't bringing glory to anyone — let alone Christ. I experienced a severe bout of the "baby blues" after each biological delivery and I figured *surely* such a thing wouldn't plague me again if the children I bore came through adoption rather than my womb. Unfortunately, I could not have been more wrong. The tears I fought so hard to keep at bay marched onto the scene unannounced at all hours of the day and night.

It was clear the life I had carefully manufactured for myself, one defined by specific and firm boundaries, wasn't working. The boundaries had been breached. By expanding our family in this way, we effectively blurred the lines between safe and predictable (at least inasmuch as any of us can claim those desired parameters) and utterly out of control. I felt stifled, trapped and hopeless. Innocent children grieved the loss of all they had ever known and so did I. How could this possibly be a win/win situation? All parts of our family seemed to float outside "original design." Kelel and Senait no longer lived with their first family and our formal family system had been shaken to the core. My soul sank heavy for each member of our tribe. Anger and frustration nestled just beneath the surface of my heart and my mind rested firmly on the trigger. My fickle flesh ruled the roost while I happily hosted a personal pity party–*corrupted* by confusion, resignation and regret. In essence, my soul lived in a restricted state, operating in the emotion *du jour*.

There was no detectable rhythm or peace. Each day brought misunderstandings that grew into all out brawls. I vigorously labored under the work of my own flesh and felt empty — dare I say, corrupted. My heart longed for a place of rest, the profound, eternal kind of rest promised in Hebrews chapter 4, *"There still remains a place of rest, a true Sabbath, for the people of God because those who enter into salvation's rest lay down their labors in the same way that God entered into a Sabbath rest from His. So let us move forward to enter this rest, so that none of us fall into the kind of faithless disobedience that prevented them from entering,"* (Hebrews 4: 9-11, The Voice).

The idea of "moving forward to enter this rest" sounded like fresh water to my parched soul. I just had trouble wrapping my mind around the fact that the very reason I wasn't experiencing this rest might be tied to my own "faithless disobedience." Hadn't it been our actual *obedience* to the Lord that brought us here in the first place? How, then, did my soul end up so *corrupted* in a place of disobedience?

Perhaps Acts 4:32 can help us shed some light on this problem: *"During those days, the entire community of believers was deeply united in heart and soul to such an extent that they stopped claiming private ownership of their possessions. Instead, they held everything in common,"* (The Voice).

Those words landed on me like a thousand bricks. I was *"claiming private ownership"* of my life. It was that simple. In my estimation, God's invitation into the journey of adoption permanently changed the trajectory of everyone's future; and I wasn't sure I liked it. God felt like a younger brother (or sister in my case!) who had busted into my bedroom without asking and read my diary or messed with my stuff; my life, my kids, my future. In effect, this "me first/mine" mentality was the portal that ushered in the very corruption against which James warned the body of believers.

On the third Sunday home from Ethiopia, Scott and I found ourselves desperate for community. In spite of any better judgment, we rallied to get everyone to church. Nothing a few lollipops in my purse couldn't handle. As we headed down the all familiar route, my mind processed the vast change up of the cast of characters in the car. Kids piled out and we not-so-silently slipped into the rear of the sanctuary, hoping against hope we could actually make it through the entire service without major disruption or incident.

We found ourselves sitting in the same place we had frequented dozens of times before, only this time everything that once felt "old hat" began to take on a life of its own. The weekly prayer of thanksgiving soaked deep in our veins and we clung to every word that came from the pastor's mouth. We searched for glimmers of hope. The same songs we had sung 100 times if we'd sung them once brought new meaning and fresh tears to our eyes. The prayer of confession...? Oh, the prayer of confession! 30 seconds wasn't nearly enough time to unload at the foot of the cross.

As we reminisce about that day, Scott recounts his personal revelation in his own words:

I was only on to my second confession when our pastor closed us in prayer. Wait! *I thought. I wasn't done. I was a mess, a wreck and I had so much more to confess. Then it dawned on me. I was the rich young ruler, the one I had read about so many times. The one I had judged and ridiculed. In that moment, I realized that I was he!*

For so many years I had been generous, as you might suggest the rich young ruler was generous. I obeyed the laws. I have always been a good, upstanding citizen. I don't swear. I don't cheat. I am honest. The list goes on... But, when we invited Kelel and Senait into

100

*our home, it exposed that my heart was, in fact, still
quite far from the Lord. King David was a knuck-
lehead in so many ways, but at the end of the day,
he was called a 'man after God's own heart' (Acts
13:22). Living in that perfect storm, that "wilderness"
if you will, revealed to me just how broken I was. It
exposed my selfishness. It unearthed my strong desire
to be comfortable, to have control over everything I
touch. As I poured out my confessions to the Lord, I
realized I had lived the life of the rich young ruler
and this journey of adoption was the first step in our
call to 'sell everything we have and give to the poor.'*

*I was and am the rich young ruler. I know what it
means to walk away because I have great wealth.*

As a couple, Scott and I had claimed "private ownership"
of our stuff. In normal, human, fleshly fashion we fancied
ourselves grateful owners of all God had given us; good stew-
ards if you will. While it is true that *"every good and perfect gift comes from the Father of Lights,"* (James 1:17) the
mental deceit took root when we figuratively transferred the
ownership and title of said gifts from "His" to "ours." Same
stuff, different attitude.

Though we had walked in faith for many years, a part of
our spiritual eyes were still blind. In that moment, however,
seated in the back row of the sanctuary, the scales fell from
our eyes. We finally began to understand, at least in a preliminary fashion, what it meant to "take up our cross" and follow
Him. Our hearts connected with Job's ancient wisdom when
he confessed to the Lord, *"I had heard about you before, but
now I have seen you with my own eyes. I take back everything
I said, and I sit in dust and ashes to show my repentance,"*
(Job 42:5-6, NLT).

Together, the Lord invited us on a journey of repentance akin to the one of which John the Baptist foretold over 2,000 years ago, *"Repent for the Kingdom of Heaven is near!"* (Matthew 3:2). This phrase would soon be Jesus' impartation as well in Matthew 4:17. Prostrate before the Lord, we repented of the sin that so easily and willingly entangled us. The sin exposed by two unlikely little souls who arrived in our home battered and broken, tossed by trauma. Every time a child recoiled from my embrace, my heart grew tired. Every word that languished under the blanket of misunderstanding cast a shadow of defeat over my soul. A spirit of despair and resignation threatened to control my thoughts. I questioned God's will and wondered if He really knew what He was doing. Did He really have this all under control?

The truth was, in my heart of hearts, I wasn't sure I trusted His control; I wanted to take it back and micro-manage it as my own. Then, any fallout would be mine, not God's. I wasn't sure how to wrap my mind around God's perfect sovereignty in this case. The utter depravity of my humanity sat on display for all to see. I snapped at those I loved the most and cried at the drop of a hat; not exactly a great formula for a thriving family. If I could see to it to lower my defenses, crucify my pride, and loosen my vice-grip on expectation, well then, I might be able to position myself to step into a place of unabashed, Christ-centered love. If I could lean into my identity as a daughter of the King and let God fill the gaping holes in my heart, we all just might stand a fighting chance.

This was not the first time I faced the corruption of my own flesh; but it was, perhaps, the first time I decided I needed to do something about it — and fast.

Chapter 9:

The Issue with Identity Issues

*"How we praise God, the Father of our Lord Jesus
Christ, who has blessed us with every spiritual
blessing in the heavenly realms because we belong
to Christ. Long ago, even before he made the world,
God loved us and chose us in Christ to be holy and
without fault in his eyes. His unchanging plan has
always been **to adopt us** into his own family by
bringing us to himself through Jesus Christ. And
this gave Him great pleasure."*

— Ephesians 1:3-5 (NLT)

Similar manifestations of grief and abandonment to those
my children exhibited (like fear, distrust and anxiety)
festered in me as well because the reality is that I too am
adopted — at least in the spiritual sense. I did not enter into
the family of God through any natural means of my own. I
am grafted in through Jesus' sacrificial death on the cross; His
sacrificial atonement for all sin. I am His child, born completely of supernatural, unmerited grace.

Honestly, I can't think of a time in my life that I truly
wrapped my mind around this concept until we brought our

kids home. Over the years, I confess I had read and absorbed these verses about spiritual adoption in a rather shallow manner. I would even venture to say I only saw in part what I am now beginning to see in whole. For as long as I can remember, I have believed God loves me — at least in the overarching sense, in the way a parent loves a child. I mean, parents are *supposed* to love their children, right? I know some species eat their young (and I'd be lying if I said that has never once crossed my mind), but as far as humans go, I'm pretty sure parents loving their children is somewhere in the original blueprint.

However, to understand that God chose me, not because He *had* to, but because He *wanted* to? Now that idea was altogether mystifying because, technically, I am not, never was and never will be adopted in the physical sense.

I grew up in a small, northern Colorado town in a 100-year-old, stone-washed brick two-story with my biological parents and younger sister. (Note reference to diary reading raid in the previous chapter. Inspired by a true story. Still haven't forgotten that one!) Throughout the years, my primary identity stemmed largely from my biological heritage. Even though I have not delved deep into any labyrinth of genealogical study, I am told my bloodlines fall somewhere in the Welsh/English/Austrian camp, although I was actually born on the Navajo reservation. My parents said it wasn't too hard to pick me out of a line-up in the hospital nursery. Go figure.

My sister and I spent many of our childhood moments together analyzing how we were naturally like (or in our teenage years *unlike*) each of our parents. My mom still loves to point out how I inherited her slightly curved pinky finger and slender calves, both traits passed down from her genetic pool, while it is clear my sister exhibits our Aunt Alice's flare for all things artistic and Dad's sentimental side (or, as my mom and I lovingly call it, "resistance to change").

There were a few blended families in our neck of the woods growing up, but quite frankly, no one talked much about adoption — at least not around me. I suppose it's possible that A. I was naively unaware of any adoption conversation; B. Any such conversation happened among adults and behind closed doors; or C. It really didn't happen at all — just like I remember it. In any case, it never occurred to me that the subject of adoption would have any direct connection with me personally. I wasn't adopted, no one in our family had been adopted and the idea that someday my future husband and I would adopt wasn't on my radar.

Adoption didn't even cross said radar until the Lord Himself planted that seed in our hearts. When Scott and I decided to open up our family planning to Him while nestled on a picnic blanket in Napa Valley, California, we were in fact offering what we considered to be a minuscule little mustard seed. A seed we ultimately ended up burying so deeply beneath the surface of our hearts it took a while for God to bring it back to our awareness.

However, from that point on (unbeknownst to us) the Lord gently watered that meager offering. As the Holy Spirit watered, the seed took root and eventually the root grew into a divine invitation to experience God's radical, unconditional love in a brand new way. I have a good friend who says, "*God is a gentleman. He will never force His plans on us.*" I find this to be indomitably true. He woos, He pursues, but it is entirely up to us how we respond to this heavenly invitation of love. Woo us and pursue us He did. The root wound its way up through the tender soil of our hearts and we ultimately got to a place where its existence was undeniable. Like children on Christmas morning, we couldn't wait to see what God actually had in store for us! We eagerly traversed this new journey of faith.

When we began to share the news of our upcoming adoption, friends and family responded in any number of ways.

More often than not, however, their response trended towards something like, *"That's amazing! You guys are awesome. Those kids will be so blessed."* In a shallow, worldly sense, I suppose one could view it that way. But, Lord have mercy! Once Kelel and Senait arrived in our home, our previously malnourished children received access to every material thing one could imagine — copious amounts of food, parasite-free drinking water, and warm showers — but they sure as heck fire did not immediately feel blessed. Even though they had what they *needed* to survive, they did not have what they *wanted*, which was to grow up with their biological family where they had previously found understanding and belonging.

In the fragility of those early days, Kelel and Senait were, for all intents and purposes, Nilsens in name only. Their identities — who they thought they were, who they believed themselves to be — had been compromised. Although their passports read "Nilsen," their hearts did not. Who could blame them? This adoption, the coming together of our family, was the bi-product of a broken world, broken bodies, broken economies and a broken system. In the midst of this understandable identity crisis, God's redemptive hand was already at work; but much like the mustard seed, it moved in mysterious ways, invisible to the naked eye.

Even under the duress of utter frustration at our children's lack of interest and distinct absence of gratitude at being part of our family, my heart ached for them. I imagined what it might have been like if I had lost both my parents at an early age. I conjured, with even broader emotion, images of what it would be like to relinquish my biological children to another's care. By all accounts, their identity crisis made total sense given the trauma they had experienced. One single stroke of a judge's pen signified all we had was also theirs, but they could not, and would not, receive it. At least not in its full form. Could this resemble my spiritual posture as well?

Even though I've been a Christian since I could reach the kitchen faucet on tip-toe, I was not living into my full identity as a daughter of Christ. I was not receiving my full spiritual inheritance. Although Christ had lived in me for the better part of my life, I still found it (and unfortunately, still do from time to time) difficult to give Him total control. Why is that? Perhaps one reason is, if I'm completely honest, that I don't trust Him implicitly to be a good and gracious Father. At the end of the day, I often wonder if He *really* has my best interests in mind. Might my desires, my life, be expendable for the greater good? This stark realization about my own lack of trust breathed newfound compassion in my soul as I thought about my kids. Just like they struggled to trust us, I also struggled to vulnerably surrender my entire being to God, and I didn't even come from a place of trauma like they did.

While adoption is a most beautiful gift, it is also a journey fundamentally born of abandonment and confusion. In fact, some adopted children experience such profound grief as a result of their keen sense of loss that they have an extremely hard, if near impossible, time attaching to their new care-givers. In those acute cases, children who come from hard places experience what psychologists term "attachment dis-order." Although I am not particularly a fan of labels, this one has been used over the years in the adoption arena and is one that, I would argue, potentially scares people away from even entertaining the idea of adoption — let alone choosing it for their family — due to an increased sense of fear that the risk involved for healthy attachment may be too great.

Fear certainly raised its ugly head, but I would submit that fear-based decision making in any area of our lives has the potential to hold us captive. Fear-based choices block the possibility of uncovering supernatural love because *fear has to do with punishment,* which is the opposite of love, whereas *"perfect love [a.k.a. God's love] casts out all fear,"* (1 John 4:18). Although fear existed, we did not and would not let it win. God's heartbeat pulsed stronger and louder than our fleshly concerns. It was not easy to soften the voice of fear, but we knew if we didn't we would be willingly declining God's invitation. We took each moment captive and ventured into the next brave step. We chose to believe God's promises for His children; promises for good and not for harm, promises of hope and a future.

Whether our faith-based actions manifest in the area of adoption or in *any* other call God has on our lives, once we agree to follow Him, we can be confident He will show up to equip us for that call. Many times, in ways we might never expect. I believe choosing to follow God at His invitation of adoption was, for us, a direct link to uncovering and discovering a beautiful new window into the Kingdom of God, one we may have missed entirely if we had not said, "Yes."

The Apostle Paul declares we can confidently say "yes" to God because He first said "yes" to us (1 John 4:19). The chicken and the egg analogy should hold no place in God's greater story. Paul explains that in our natural, sinful, born-of-this-world state, we were utterly helpless to save ourselves. Though knitted together in our mother's womb we were, in effect, spiritually fatherless, *"but God showed His great love for us by sending Christ to die for us while we were still sinners,"* (Romans 5:18). He adopted us — warts and all — and grafted us into His family. We who were once fully dead in our sin (not just "mostly dead" like Billy Crystal's prognosis of our hero Wesley in the movie *The Princess Bride*) are now brought into new life, into a new family, through the final, sacrificial, atonement of God's own son, Jesus Christ. That is an identity changer, indeed!

For years there was a part of me that operated under a self-imposed hierarchy of acceptance. I believed in order to truly fit in and be liked, I needed to perform in a certain way. I've always been a people pleaser of the highest order. At my parents' very first parent/teacher conference, my pre-school teacher told them, "Megan is a delightful little girl. A real pleasure to have in class. But please let her know that she can get her hands dirty. She doesn't need to be so worried about being perfect."

Perhaps I can blame some of that on my first-born status, but those excuses only go so far. For some reason, my identity became wrapped up in what others thought of me, and I figured they'd only really like me if I succeeded in life — that somehow perceived success would make me likable. In some strange way, I suppose I was jealous of those people who exuded confidence and seemed to know exactly who they were. I didn't know how to live free and confident in my own skin; believing God had created me just as He wanted and that was more than good enough.

The word "adoption" literally means "to choose." The Latin root *ad* means "to" and *option* means "choosing." Merriam Webster further defines adoption as the "act or process of giving official acceptance or approval to something." Imbedded in the very root of the word is the idea of radical, unconditional, desired, covenantal *choice* to acceptance and love. The very nature of adoption communicates that you and I are wanted; you and I belong. Our primary identities no longer lie in the temporary, counterfeit, shallow offerings of this world. I am not merely a mother, sister, daughter, friend, writer or mediocre cook — rather, I am first and foremost a child of the King! (Spoiler alert: So are you!) Once I find myself firmly grounded on that foundational principle, everything else — who I am and what I do — can flow directly from that place.

This same truth applies to anyone in the body of Christ. The instant we find ourselves in Christ, "*the old has gone and the new has come,*" (2 Corinthians 5:17). We are children of the King; wholly and dearly loved (Colossians 3:12). I don't care if you have adopted children, plan to adopt someday or wouldn't entertain the idea of adoption in your wildest dreams... I don't care if you were raised by your biological parents, adopted into a natural family somewhere along the way, or if you were raised in a barn! The truth is, if you are in Christ you are an adopted child, and this life-altering fact changes everything.

Who we once *were*, is not now who we *are*. The question is: Are we ready to accept it? Not just in part, but in full? Do you find comfort in your old skin, however bound and broken it may be? Or, by faith, are you ready to shed your old nature and confidently put on the new?

Ephesians 2:1-3 (NLT) tells us:

Once you were dead, doomed forever because of your many sins. You used to live just like the rest of the world, full of sin, obeying Satan, the mighty prince of the power of the air. He is the spirit at work in the hearts of those who refuse to obey God. All of us used to live that way, following the passions and desires of our evil nature. We were born with an evil nature, and we were under God's anger like everyone else.

This passage describes who we *were*: dead, doomed, full of sin, refusing to obey God. This is not the identity God meant for us to have when He created man in His image for the express purpose of being in relationship with Him.

Thank goodness this is not the end of the story! Nipping at the heels of this dark description, the following verses paint an entirely different picture. Ephesians 2:4-10 (NLT) reveals a greater reality; one that, if absorbed into our mental and emotional souls, has the ability to change our posture and confidence from this day forward.

God is so rich in mercy, and He loved us so very much, that even while we were dead because of our sins, He gave us life when He raised Christ from the dead.

(It is only by God's special favor that you have been saved!) For He raised us from the dead along with Christ, and we are seated with Him in the heavenly realms — all because we are one with Christ. And so God can always point to us as examples of the incredible wealth of His favor and kindness towards us, as shown in all He has done for us through Christ Jesus.

God saved you by his special favor when you believed. And you can't take credit for this; it is a gift from God. Salvation is not a reward for the good things we have done, so none of us can boast about it. For we are God's masterpiece. He created us anew in Christ Jesus, so that we can do the good things He planned for us long ago.

These life-giving words describe who we *are*: loved, alive, favored, seated in heavenly realms, one with Christ, God's masterpiece, destined to do good things Are you kidding me? I can get on board with that identity! Let's just take a moment and allow the profound nature of this reality to sink in. You and I are God's beloved children. It is possible to live loved and be loved, *"because He first loved us,"* (1 John 4:19). We are, by nature of His grace and mercy, God's adopted children, *"...the true children of Abraham. You are his heirs, and now all the promises God gave to him belong to you,"* (Galatians 3:29).

Kelel and Senait are now Nilsens. Just as I am in God's family, they are in our family — forever and always. All that we have and all that we are, finite and fallible as we may be, now belongs to them. Any legacy, inheritance and identity we have to offer are theirs. Just as Reese and Brynn are our children, so are Kelel and Senait, whether they understand it or not. In the same way, you and I are children of God. All that He is and all that He has now belongs to us; even better,

111

resides inside of us *"...because the Spirit who lives in me is greater than the spirit who lives in the world,"* (1 John 4:14). His promises aren't encumbered by limited human frailty. His inheritance is eternal and true, beyond the bounds of anything we can think or imagine (Ephesians 3:20). Let's just try to out-dream God! Not gonna happen.

To embrace this radical, life-changing, posture-altering identity is to cast out all *natural fear* and replace it with *supernatural love.* Ultimately, Scott and I did not choose to adopt our children out of a place of fear, but out of love and faith that God can and will redeem all circumstances. Although fear crept in when the rug felt like it was pulled out from under us in those first months together, I knew fear would not have the final word. I just couldn't quite see how an alternative hope would emerge. I questioned how the light could possibly break through what seemed like impenetrable darkness. Love had to win. It just had to! Therefore, in the midst of very real fear, we chose love. It was clear we couldn't muster the feeling in our natural strength. On our knees, faces prostrate before the Lord, we asked Him to implant His supernatural love in our hearts.

The distinction here is a pivotal paradigm shift because it is only through the manifestation of love that true healing can begin. In the book, *Beyond Consequences, Logic and Control: A Love-Based Approach to Helping Children with Severe Behaviors,* author, licensed social worker and adoptive mom Heather Forbes shares her own journey in this area:

After making a paradigm shift from fear to love, not only did change become a reality, but also healing began. Healing for all family members became possible. Now looking back, it amazes me, and it is painfully difficult to ponder how we as people born of love easily lose our way to fear. How did I begin from a place of love only to find myself literally trembling in

fear and sorrow? ... Love really is enough when it is
given in the absence of fear.

I believe Heather's words to be profoundly true, not only
in a physical sense, but in a spiritual sense as well. Love
offered in the absence of fear, without expectation or strings
attached, has the capability to change everything. Even
though life's bumps, bruises and unorthodox circumstances
will naturally infuse us with some amount of fear, it is possible to exchange that fear for love; and the highest kind of
love comes from our Heavenly Father. Only His supernatural love is able to cast out all fear and replace it with our
true identity. When we know *who* we are and *whose* we are,
we can start to walk upright and free. Isn't that a beautiful
exchange?

Just as our children are our children no matter what, you
and I are God's children, no matter what! When I finally
and wholly understood, absorbed and believed this truth, my
perspective shifted. Of course, I am still a mom, wife, sister
and friend. I have hopes, dreams and personal interests. I
like skiing and chocolate. I don't like mountain biking or
olives. I like pizza, musical theater, and "Seinfeld" re-runs.
Some of these things will remain true of me until the Lord
takes me home and others might shift depending on the state
of my knee joints or the amount of money in my wallet, but
no matter the variation of season or the change of circumstance, who I am at the core of my being will never deviate. I.
Am. His. Who I am is not dictated by what I do. (Or, for that
matter, don't do.) However, what I *choose* to do absolutely
flows out of who I am.

It has taken many months of replacing fear with love for
our children and me to find and live into our true identities.
The decisive transition from relatively unhealthy patterns of
behavior to healthier standard operating procedures manifested when I started focusing less on the children's "issues"

and decided to recognize, name and repent of the very real fear that lived in me. The potential to achieve my own victory rested squarely on me. I found it alarmingly easy to unpack, analyze, and obsess about my children's fears. The fork in the road, however, came when I realized I harbored some of those exact same feelings of fear, anxiety, and worry. In Robert Frost theology, taking the road "less traveled," choosing hope over doubt, faith over fear, and love over anger has made all the difference.

Learning to breathe first and react second is the goal. Every sideways glance or defiant response from any child of mine does not have to send me over the edge and into a downward spiral as I vie for ultimate control. The reality is that I cannot control my kids (Darn it all!), just like I can't really control any relationship in my life. At least, I shouldn't. In fact, if I face each challenge from a place of confidence and peace, knowing I am deeply and totally loved no matter what, the outcome of said challenge doesn't have to scare or overwhelm me. This may sound like the most elementary of lessons, my dear Watson, but I'm not kidding when I say that just this minor tweak in perspective has revolutionized my relationship with my kids and transformed me into a much happier and peaceful mama. (Okay, okay. Not all the time. Baby steps...) At every turn, I have a choice in how I react. I can choose to operate from a place of fear and doubt or a place of love and trust.

Heather Forbes and her colleague B. Bryan Post submit, *"There are only two primary emotions: Love and Fear."* They assert:

> *Our belief is that many of the things we do are based on and driven by our understanding. The things we do are not done to be mean or intentionally cruel, but are done from the perception and understanding within us. ... Poets for centuries have attempted to define*

love. The reality is that you cannot adequately define the experience of love. The moment you have defined it, it becomes something else — that which you have defined. I have found one of the best ways to consider love is to understand that love is what we bring to the space that surrounds us. Love is not possessive or controlling. It simply exists in the present space and time. Any two people are capable of experiencing love at any given moment if they are able to put aside their fears and preconceived notions for what love is supposed to be. Love is being fully present in the moment.

To be a person that is fully present in the moment has plagued my natural, first-born DNA since birth. I am a planner — moves and countermoves. My philosophy is usually to try to stay one step ahead of the present moment in a vain attempt to avoid any potential pitfalls or perceived failure. As strange as it may sound, to live in the present is rather counterintuitive for me. However, if I don't want to be a resounding gong or a clanging symbol, I must continually choose to repent of fear and operate from a place of love. Exchanging fear for love creates something divinely wonderful. Love-over-fear living is indeed a *beautiful exchange*.

True freedom exists at the point of ultimate surrender. When I surrender my own agenda and let the Lord's plans fill my heart, I am able to live into His highest call for my life. When I operate in my highest call — this is to say, investing the talents God gave me for the glory of His name — my identity becomes abundantly clear. I no longer need to bow to the expectations of others. I only submit to the soft, sweet whisper of His Spirit. He speaks. I listen. (At least, that's the goal!) Every move and countermove now filters through the lens of the Holy Spirit. In each moment, I must ask myself if my reactions smell of fear or speak of love. This question alone takes up enough brain-space to keep me grounded in the present moment. I no longer desire to jump ahead of the game. The only fear I want to influence me is a holy one; a reverent fear of the Father. A fear that if I don't live in the divine invitation of the present, I will miss what God has planned just for me in that moment and beyond, because His plans are infinitely better than anything I could ask or imagine.

Oh, may we spur one another on to seek true freedom, the kind of freedom that only comes through holy surrender to a loving Father. I, for one, don't want to settle for anything less! If we live in such a manner, perhaps those in our sphere of influence will see the absolute joy in that way of living and follow suit. Whether we are CEO or PTO should be secondary to our first and primary calling — which is to live and move and have our being as beloved children of the most High King. Once we operate from the freedom of that place, everything else — from the daily tasks to our soul's true calling — will fall into place. (I'm not submitting this will always be easy, but it will always be good!) Redemption, for mind, body and soul won't be far behind.

Chapter 10:

Redemption Song

*"To be able to look backward and say, 'This has
been the finest year of my life' — that is glorious!
But anticipation! To be able to look ahead and say,
'The present year can and shall be better!' — that
is more glorious! If we said such things about our
achievements, we would be consummate egoists.
But if we are speaking of God's kindness, and we
speak truly, we are but grateful. And this is what
I do witness. I have done nothing but open windows — God has done all the rest.'"*

— *Frank Laubach*, Practicing His Presence

It was precisely in the vortex of our collective mess that
God's grace and mercy picked up the scattered pieces of
our lives and began tenderly weaving the frayed threads of
our souls into a beautiful tapestry. The vulnerable exposure of
weak flesh we experienced in those early days together liber-
ated our souls to the point of sheer dependence on Him and,
in so doing, released the Spirit of God to move on with the
business at hand, the business in which He specializes — that
is the business of redemption.

Of course, the one-time-only, it-is-finished, glory-halle-lujah, heaven-bound redemption transpired at the cross. I am square on that. However, as the passionate Greek-Australian preacher, Christine Caine declares, "Don't just live *delivered* when you can live *free!*" I believe she crafted those words with the express intent of hitting the heart of a person like me. Delivered for the life to come, but not truly free in this one.

I now sense the compelling rush of uncharted waters. The tide is turning, God's presence is rising, and I am but a spiritual babe in arms. What I thought I knew about life and love feels like a mere seed that only recently sprouted from infancy. Our testimony, though more real than anything I've experienced to this point, remains a grand mystery of sorts. How does one begin to describe to another's kindred soul the vast breadth, depth and love of the Father? Is it even possible to wrap mortal words around an immortal, divine encounter? I don't really know, but I cannot rest until I give it a proper try.

It is clear to me even on my best day that I, myself, have done and can do nothing of eternal substance. Eternal significance can only be achieved through the grace and redemptive blood of Jesus Christ. The apostle John proclaims we will *"overcome by the blood of the Lamb and the word of our testimony,"* (Revelation 12:11), so I will do just that. I will open the windows of testimony to proclaim that God really has done all the rest.

Window No. 1: Our Kids Were Not, Are Not and Never Will Be, the Enemy

"For we are not fighting against people made of flesh and blood, but against the evil rulers and authorities of the unseen world, against those mighty powers of darkness who rule this world, and against wicked spirits in the heavenly realms." (Ephesians 6:12, NLT)

When we arrived home, Scott and I felt like all hell had broken loose (quite literally as we would later discover) and we were powerless against its wrath. Understandably, our children grieved the loss of their first family as well as their motherland. Their emotions raged like the waves of an angry sea and I felt caught in the undercurrent. The trauma of being ripped from the only home they'd ever known manifested differently in each child, but erupted in one difficult behavior or another nevertheless.

I keenly remember one frosty December morning during that first month at home. I felt trapped and decided a trip to our local Ross store would provide a little affordable retail therapy. The glaring fluorescent lights and hoards of Christmas shoppers would have kept me away in any other season of life, but on that day I fancied the distraction a welcome reprieve. Ultimately, I never even made it inside the front door.

No sooner did I pull into a parking spot and command myself to "just breathe," than I turned to find that a dear friend had pulled up beside me with her two little ones in tow. Jenny hadn't seen us since we'd been home, but whispers of our delicate emotional state spread like wildfire in our close-knit community.

She greeted me with open arms, "Megan!! So good to see you. How are you?!"

"Hey…Jenny!" I stammered.

Her warm hug and friendly words cracked my hard-fought defenses. I tried to look away as tears streamed down my cheeks. I couldn't hide behind the staid, "Everything is fine — *really!*" facade. I'd been made — the frog in my throat blocked any other attempt at coherent communication. Her spirit instantly connected with mine. In the midst of our tearful embrace, my girlfriend recounted the vision God gave her that very morning.

"I can't believe we ran into each other like this. Well, I guess I can…" she smiled. "This morning, as I was worshipping, God brought your family to my mind. I saw your house with countless people around it. Some folks I recognized and some I didn't. He showed me a group with their faces lifted towards heaven, pleading and interceding to the Lord on your behalf."

She thought for a moment. "Just now, when I laid eyes on you, the vision became clear. We need to come to your house to pray."

That very morning, she circulated this email among our family and friends,

You probably just read Megan's email about their "state of affairs" and the spiritual battle they are engaged in. After reading it, Eugene and I felt burdened to pray as a group of believers, the body of Christ.

We wanted to get as close to them as possible without disturbing their household, so we thought of the park adjacent to their house as a great spot to gather.

Will you join us with your family this afternoon in praying for the Nilsens? We will be meeting at the park, so if you bring your kids they can play while we pray. We will meet at 4pm and pray fervently that the Lord would intervene and that the Holy Spirit would be present on the Nilsen's circumstances.

That cold December afternoon, the bitter wind wasn't the only battle our friends braved. They huddled together in a holy circle. With fingers interlocked and faces exposed to the elements, a faith-filled army raised prayers heavenward and interceded on our behalf. Men, women and children pleaded with the Lord to rebuke any lingering demons of distrust and fear — in all of us.

Throughout the months that followed, we invited a number of people to pray in and around our home, not the least of which were several African nationals and fellow Young Life staff who were on a fundraising tour throughout the US. The Spirit and anointing they carried into our home is something I will not soon forget. In Jesus' name we decreed and declared God's promises of light and freedom, hope and peace and, pretty please, a good night's sleep over our house.

Our children had come to us from a place of trauma. The words "voluntary relinquishment" meant *abandonment* to our sweet kids and "failure to provide" really meant *failure to thrive* — in all senses of the word. Knowing full well our delicate yet resilient kids were not the enemy, I wrote a poem about my relationship with Kelel in an effort to process our complicated and layered new world:

He is afraid of forgetting. Forgetting the mother he loves, his mother country and his mother tongue.

How can he love two people at once? Two places at once? It seems impossible to his eight-year-old mind.

His fight is strong. The protector, his namesake, comes out in force. His eyes grow dark and his tongue spits venom. Words aimed to wound land like arrows in the night.

The fight is strong. But love is stronger.

Love's vice grip leans in a little tighter. A little fiercer. A righteous love that will never give up. Never give in.

121

A raging sea of emotion thrashes in his heart.

Every time a memory begins to fade, his body reacts. Holding tight to a loyal love means pushing away another. The two seem mutually exclusive.

Or are they?

Minutes tick away, leading into more than an hour. And then, just as quickly as it starts and rapidly escalates, the fight begins to fade.

Ever so slightly, bodies relax. Eyes closed tight gradually flicker open. The semblance of a smile starts to form on the sides of his mouth. My clenched jaw softens. So does his.

"Honey, are you afraid you can't love two mommies at once?"

Hesitantly, "Yes."

And so it goes. We gingerly enter into a sacred dance. A routine relegated only for the most intimate of people. A place where the dark night of the soul and life's truest freedom dare to co-exist.

I explain to him that not only can he love two mommies at once — the two of us metaphorically intertwine to form one heart. My heart bends into hers and we are forever connected in a shape that symbolizes true love to all who dare to dream of such things.

122

Not only do the two of us form the core, One greater forms the shell.

Inside a Jesus-shaped heart, we can fit the whole world. A Jesus-shaped heart stretches into supernatural infinity and beyond. Because He died, offering His heart, splayed for the taking, we can take up residence.

The confines of a finite world are broken. The boundaries of time and space begin to shatter.

A Jesus-shaped heart fits all of us. The ones we are beginning to remember and the ones we are starting to forget.

She and I are inextricably one.

Her blood courses through your veins while my hands caress your face.

Your eyes reflect her voracious love while mine reflect it right back.

May you never forget.

May I always remember.

Inside our Jesus-shaped space.

The confines of earthly geometry tend to stifle the shape of the Holy Spirit. When we recognize our deepest battle is not against flesh and blood, but against the powers of darkness, the shape of the fight begins to change. It is only as we accurately perceive and recognize the shape of the true battle that we can take proper action, for the war is won, but the battle rages on. This may sound like overly-dramatic "*Lord of the Rings*" talk here, but it's true! The gravity of our fallen world's sphere only serves to limit the abundance and freedom found in an eternal, ethereal Jesus-shaped space.

This type of love is a gorgeously complex thing to navigate because I am not Kelel and Senait's first mommy, nor their first love. God wove their inner-most beings inside the womb of another and, because of a broken and complicated system, their days will not play out under her watchful eye. It seems entirely and utterly unfair at best. Why me and not her? I will most likely never know the answer to that question this side of heaven. Even though I cannot wrap my mind around the layered nuances of this truth, it is a reality nevertheless. When God brought Kelel and Senait into our home, He also extended our family ties far beyond our local borders. Although this can be confusing at times, it provides one more window into the vast expanse of the love of God.

Many times, this duality of motherhood brings with it an inherent battle for control — quite often in my own heart. When my kids bristle under the words of my authority, my first instinct is to ramp up the "control-o-meter." I want to speak more forcefully, make them look me in the eye. I have been known to shout or grab an arm. (Oh, how I regret those moments.) Often, just a sideways glare, a dismissive shoulder shrug or a wry cackle from any of my children can launch me into a battle of wills in a heartbeat.

However, in that moment, I have two choices. I can pick up that offense, march it straight to the proverbial "mom bank" and deposit it in the mental account labeled, "you-need-to-listen-to-me-because-I'm-your-mother" (a frequent choice of mine, by the way). Or, I can decide to die to my fleshly nature and insatiable need for control and follow Jesus. Following Him in that moment simply means that I take a breath (yes — this is seriously a step for me!) and pray a quick prayer for God's Spirit of patience, wisdom and creativity to wash over me. I exchange my need to control for His Spirit of love. This beautiful exchange provides much needed perspective so I (hopefully) avoid the major mommy crash and burn that plagues me more often than I care to admit — for those who *"love God's law have great peace and do not stumble,"* (Psalm 119:165).

Author Francis Frangipane suggests:

In the battles of life, your peace is actually a weapon ... You see, the first step toward having spiritual authority over the adversary is having peace in spite of our circumstances. When Jesus confronted the devil, He did not confront Satan with His emotions or in fear. Knowing that the devil was a liar, He simply refused to be influenced by any other voice than God's. His peace overwhelmed Satan, His authority then shattered the lie, which sent demons fleeing.

When I'm faced with the tension of everyday moments — you know, the ones that can sneak up on you like your mother-in-law's birthday — I have found the only key to true inner peace is to embrace Jesus' complete confidence in His place of honor and authority as the Father's Son. Heaven knows I don't always get this right the first time! My prayer and petition from this day forward is that I learn to recalibrate more quickly every single time, because the truth is that in the abundantly extravagant economy of the Kingdom, I can afford it.

I'm not actually giving up control; rather, I rightfully transfer control *back* to the One who ultimately laid down His life for me so I could do the same.

Window No. 2: Recognizing Small Victories Ultimately Reaps Big Reward

First steps, however timid, are exciting. I remember when our oldest learned to walk. Of course, the natural order of events preceded those preliminary steps. Baby Reese flashed a gummy grin right around 8 weeks of age. He rolled over at 4 months, sat unassisted at 6 months, mastered the commando army crawl like he was avoiding stray shrapnel around 7 months, and embraced a new sense of freedom when he began to scurry on all fours shortly thereafter. Just before his first birthday, he spent numerous hours crawling to the nearest chair or coffee table. Once there, he would reach his little hands towards the flat surface, muster all the strength he could in those chubby little arms of his and hoist himself up onto his feet.

For several weeks, he walked in circles around the coffee table, hands grape-vining their way around the perimeter, providing stability to curious feet that followed. The repetition of those movements moved into mastery, which in turn boosted his bouncing baby confidence. In fact, he mustered up so much swagger that, at 12-months of age, he was ready to pivot 180 degrees and look out onto the great abyss of the living room from about the same vantage point as our surly yellow lab, as if the space were something he too might conquer one day.

If Scott or I happened to be seated a few feet away, a smile of recognition would flash across Reese's face. Our presence provided the assurance he needed to take this skill to the next level, and we encouraged him to take the risk. We would look intently into his lake-blue eyes, extend our hands, and beckon him into our arms, "Come on, buddy! You can do it! There you go... You've got this!" Often, he'd take a step, teeter backwards, and land flat on his diapered rump. "That's okay," we'd coo. "Try again. We've got you!" And so it went until, one day, he actually bumbled his way across the room. We cheered like he'd just been awarded the National Medal of Honor. Our hearts combusted with parental pride. Surely, he was a freak of nature, a walking prodigy, we marveled. Surely.

So it goes with the redemptive movement of God. Beauty and redemption don't usually manifest overnight. Of course, they can because our God is a God of radical, blow-your-mind miracles, but more often than not, redemption is worked out in the great expanse of the journey. In the timid first steps. In the risks and the failures and the try-agains until we arrive on the other side and recognize the beautifully redemptive moment as one that encapsulates all the hard-fought victories along the way.

Remember how I mentioned our kids didn't speak English when we first met them? Yeah. That was…how do you say…? Brutal. Challenging. Extremely frustrating for all parties. We didn't know any Tigrinya and they didn't know any English, save for words like "No!" Which actually meant, "Hell, no." I, for one, kind of freaked out under the weight of not being able to communicate. I rifled through our junk drawers in search of some 3x5 cards I originally intended to use for recipes. They were still blank. "I know they're in here somewhere…." I muttered.

Sure enough, beneath the dried up pens and stray pencil shavings I found a handful of little white index cards. I scanned the house and started writing down the names of the household items I saw around me in big block letters. LAMP. CURTAIN. MICROWAVE. COUCH. CHAIR. TABLE. WINDOW. REFRIGERATOR. Scratch that, too long, just FRIDGE. And so on. I taped these cards to the corresponding item as if somehow my kids would magically learn to read and absorb the words and their meanings with their prodigious photographic memories. Chalk that up as "not so successful" on a scale of ridiculous ideas born out of desperation.

The bumpy road towards communication consisted of spontaneous, made-up sign language for quite some time.

"Do you want to eat…?" I'd ask as I dropped my jaw into the shape of a wide operatic oval and lifted my hand to my mouth like I was slurping a bowl of minestrone.

"Time for a bath!" I'd sing, lifting one arm and pretending to wash my armpit with an imaginary washcloth.

"Bedtime!" was always accompanied by a wide stretch of the arms and an exaggerated yawn. I would tilt my head to one side, close my eyes and slide my hands, with palms pressed together, under my head to signal the end of the day.

I was always hopeful that somehow each new night might usher in an easier bedtime routine, that somehow on that particular night I wouldn't need to lay down with each child until they finally gave up the fight and succumbed to much-needed sleep. Each time, I was disappointed. Night after night, hour by hour, we shuffled a pint-sized Senait back into her own bed until one morning, we woke up and realized neither of us remembered any interruptions.

I can't tell you exactly when we started to slide into a routine, a "new normal" if you will. It just sort of happened. Slowly but surely, English words replaced Tigrinya words. In fact, it wasn't long before Kelel and Senait started speaking to each other only in English. Unfortunately, neither one had any clear mastery of their newfound English-speaking tongues, which often resulted in even more bickering.

"Just speak to each other in Tigrinya! It would be so much easier," I'd plead.

To which Kelel would reply, "Tigrinya is Tigrinya!" Oh brother. Eventually, however, rudimentary language emerged and once impossible communication morphed into a stunted jumble of words. With each small victory we clapped and cheered and nodded our heads enthusiastically, "Yes! Yes! Eeeggg. Do you want one or two?"

"Four!" Kelel would insist. Sure enough, he could scarf down at least three or four eggs, two bananas and a bag of popcorn in less than the time it took for him to grab another bag of popcorn and throw it into the microwave. Before I had a chance to protest, I would see the bag spinning inside the machine and hear the *pop, pop, pop* of more comfort food.

As the months progressed, I glimpsed sweet and tender moments between our kids as well. Dinnertime was often followed by an all-out four-kid chase around the kitchen island while Scott and I loaded the dishwasher. Although these moments dotted many harder ones, the hooting and howling of a happy nature was music to my ears, no matter how fleeting.

Kelel and Senait resisted books for a long time. They were not accustomed to them and, much to my dismay, didn't care to give the ones we tried to read at bedtime a second glance. One night, however, as I approached the top of the stairs, braced for the usual nighttime drama, I realized it was actually kind of quiet. I peeked my head into the girls' room and witnessed Brynn, with board book in hand, animatedly repeating, "Five little monkeys jumping on the bed! One fell off and broke his head..." Kelel and Senait sat rapt, soaking in each repetition of this ridiculous and funny story. Oh, the small victories! The day I saw Reese bend down to scoop up Senait's hand and tenderly help her across the icy driveway, I wanted to stop time in its tracks and just soak in the moment. These mental snapshots are beyond precious. I log them in my memory bank and don't take even a single one for granted.

There seems to be a natural progression to redemption that mirrors the journey of life itself. A garden does not sprout into full bloom at the blink of an eye, but gradually, with each passing day, consistent love waters infant seeds of trust. Light streams in to nourish the garden through a random hug, a gentle smile, a shared cup of hot chocolate or proud recognition of success. And just like a baby begins to walk, so our relationships started to bloom — taking on a sweet smell and vibrant life of their own. Of course, this garden continues to undergo the natural cycle of pruning, dormancy and harvest-time even today, but now I see hope and redemption in brilliant Technicolor where it once was doubt-ridden and dim.

Window No. 3: The Kingdom of Heaven is not "What" or "Where," but "Who"

The inception of our adoption journey triggered an insatiable need inside my soul, a desire to hunt down the Kingdom of Heaven like an ancient explorer doggedly searching for a new world. I knew it was there. I'd heard tales from others, but I hadn't totally experienced it for myself and I desperately wanted that to change.

As it was, the Kingdom of Heaven sat before me, behind me, around me and in me the whole time. How was it possible, after so many years of walking with the Lord, that I didn't recognize nor understand how to access the manifest presence of the Holy Spirit — the third person of the trinity, the one who rounds out the complete picture of the Kingdom of Heaven? To me, the Holy Spirit was an enigma I believed existed, but with whom I wasn't sure how to relate, perhaps because I draped bright yellow *Caution* tape around my heart. Fear of true intimacy and vulnerability denied Him full access. I continue to learn, however, that I don't need to dig like a frantic puppy trying to unearth a bone; rather, I must transfer my thinking, in an act of repeated repentance, and allow the Kingdom to grow in me. I don't need to "find it," I just need to water what is already there.

In Matthew 13:32-34, Jesus compares the Kingdom of Heaven to a "mustard seed planted in a field" or "yeast used by a woman making bread." He claims the mustard seed is the *"smallest of all seeds, but becomes the largest of garden plants and grows into a tree where birds can come and find shelter in its branches"* and the *"yeast permeates every part of the dough."*

This seed, this yeast if you will, is the person of the Holy Spirit planted in me, growing me as a person, and permeating every part of me. Just like Jesus promised in John 14, the Holy Spirit has come to be my counselor, comforter, advocate and friend. He leads me as He led Jesus and my soul is His dwelling place. As I learn to walk in Him (yes, teetering and landing flat on my rump, many days), I will not so quickly *"gratify the desires of the flesh. For the desires of the flesh are against the Spirit, and the desires of the Spirit are against the flesh, for these are opposed to each other, to keep you from doing the things you want to do,"* (Galatians 5:16-17).

Now, I believe the things that I *want* to do actually mirror more of the heart of God. I want to engage in nothing short of the unique assignments He has for me. Imagine the freedom that exists when the two become one!

No. 4: Not Only Are our Kids *Not* the Enemy, our Kids Are a Window into a Kingdom Teeming with Scandalous Love and Relentless Pursuit of the "One"

The redemptive work of Jesus is, quite frankly, beyond the full scale of my comprehension. At times, I am overwhelmed by the profound brokenness of this world and don't understand how God could ultimately redeem *any* of it. The sheer magnitude of children who desperately need loving care, nourishment, and a place of unconditional belonging engulfs me. I believe God's first and most perfect design is that they would grow up in the context of their biological families but, for various reasons, that cannot always happen. A full-scale revelation of this reality ravaged me like a freight train when we arrived in Ethiopia. I didn't (and really still don't) know how to reconcile this reality in my head. However God, in His mercy, spoke to me in the night.

Every so often God reaches in and speaks to me in the form of a dream. Yes, a literal middle-of-the-night type of dream. I actually dream almost every night, but most of my dreams are the kind that seem completely lucid in the moment, but dissolve into utter nonsense when I describe the play-by-play to a very polite (but clearly bored) husband in the morning. This time the dream was different. When I woke up, heart-beating out of my chest, I knew God had a message for me. I just needed to figure out what it was. After three full days nervously laughing and playing with Kelel, Senait and virtually all the other kids at the care center in Addis Ababa, Scott and I fell into bed, anxious to reach a deep sleep so our minds and bodies could reset and get ready to receive whatever the next day might bring.

That night, however, God reached in and implanted this dream:

I was bathing a group of kids in an extremely large tub, about the size of one of those blue, plastic swimming pools someone might have in their backyard — the kind you have to climb a rickety ladder dangling on the edge to get into. As I was bathing these children I panicked because, all of a sudden, I looked around and could not find Senait anywhere. Hadn't she been happily swimming near me just a moment ago? I thrashed my arm around the tub. Sudsy water splashed everywhere. I felt a little body like dead weight, anchored to the bottom and I yanked it out. It was Senait. She was limp and lifeless. I threw her, tummy first, over my left arm. I pounded on her back with the palm of my right hand until she coughed out a stream of water lodged deep inside. At once, she began to sob as her tiny arms clung to my neck.

I awoke suddenly, breathing heavily and blinked my eyes, disoriented. It took me a moment to recall my surroundings before my brain reactivated. *What might have sparked this dream?* I wondered. What was the Lord trying to say to me?

I grabbed my journal and a pen in an attempt to sift through my thoughts.

Upon arriving in Addis Ababa, my heart sank at the overwhelming number of kids — little, teeny, tiny children wandering the streets vigilantly searching for water and food. Barefoot boys and girls tried to sell me a piece of gum or a plastic trinket whenever our car came to a stop. "One penny?" They pleaded. "Please, miss, please." Children carried babies on their hips because many were, in fact, the chief guardians of the younger ones.

How could one adoption make an ounce of difference in this vast sea of need? Their needs put my perceived needs to shame. In America, I "need" to call a repairman to fix a leaky roof. These kids needed a roof for shelter alone. I "need" to buy drinks for a party I'm hosting on a Saturday night. These kids just needed a drink of water to live — pure, clean water at that. The reality of this disparity overwhelmed me, but that's exactly when God spoke.

Through my nightmare, He reminded me that, though He loves all, His heart continually beats for the *one*. The forgotten one. The one who wanders the street alone. The one who needs a home. The one who needs to find water, food and love — true, unconditional, selfless love. The words of Matthew 18:10-14 flooded my heart.

*See that you do not look down on **one** of these little ones. For I tell you that their angels in heaven always see the face of my Father in heaven. What do you think? If a man owns a hundred sheep and one of them wanders away, will he not leave the ninety-nine on the hills and go to look for the **one** that wandered off? And if he finds it, I tell you the truth, he is happier about that **one** sheep than about the ninety-nine that did not wander off. In the same way, your Father*

*in heaven is not willing that any of these little ones
should be lost.* [emphasis mine]

Could it be the God of the universe, the One who sees all
and knows all, actually sees each one of us? He sees my sweet
children. He sees me and He sees you. This life is not com-
partmentalized into "either/or," but rather "both/and." We are
all "the one." He loved and always will love me enough to
invite me into this call of adoption — a unique call which
draws me ever closer to His heart. He loves me enough to use
the most precious in His sight to soften my heart, completing
a grander picture of His Kingdom, expanding the amount of
love flowing through these walls to greater levels than I could
have ever imagined.

He loves you just the same. He is absolutely nuts about
you! Do you want more of Him? I'm pretty darn sure He
wants more of you. What crazy journey might God be inviting
you to take because He knows the endgame is deeper peace,
joy, and intimacy with Him? I don't understand the supernatural mathematics of it all. At the end of the day, the numbers
don't balance out. With each touch, each smile, each small
victory, if you will, the "least of these" are actually saving me.
Scott and I have not necessarily changed our children; rather,
our children have changed us.

In retrospect, I suppose it shouldn't come as any surprise
that the Kingdom of Heaven would break into our lives in
conjunction with the arrival of two young children. After all,
just before Jesus chastised the rich young ruler, *"Some children were brought to Jesus so He could lay hands on them
and pray for them. The disciples rebuked them. But Jesus said,
'Let the children come to me, and do not hinder them, for
the kingdom of heaven belongs to such as these,'"* (Matthew
9:13-14, NLT). Little did we know, in what felt like a dark
night of the soul, that God's breath of redemption hovered

over the waters, awakening us to new revelation — of ourselves and of Him.

Once again, Christine Caine says it best, *"Knowing our true identity is only half the battle; once we know it, we have to guard it."*

Chapter 11:

On Earth as it is in Heaven (a.k.a. A Beautiful Exchange)

*"If our destiny is to grow on and on and on, into
some far more beautiful creatures than we are now,
that means that we need to have the shells broken
quite frequently **so that we can grow**."*

— *Frank Laubach,* Practicing His Presence

E ternal destiny. Increasing beauty. Continuous growth.
Doesn't that describe a bit of heaven here on earth? Love
it. Sign me up! At the end of the day, doesn't this encapsulate
what so many of us want? The Westminster Catechism, dating
back to 1647, claims, *"The chief end of man is to glorify God
and enjoy Him forever."* Again, no hard sell here. I could day-
dream *ad-nauseam* about the "new heaven and the new earth"
described in the book of Revelation. Not sure how I feel
about the tribulation and such in between, but heaven? I'm in.

If King Solomon was right and God *"set eternity in the
hearts of men"* (Ecclesiastes 3:11), it stands to reason that
somewhere deep inside our souls we long for the future abundance and promise of heaven as we march onward; desiring

to *"live and move and have our being,"* (Acts 17:28) in sync with heaven's holy rhythm. We might not be able to put words to this guttural longing, yet we nod our heads in agreement. No more sorrow. No more tears. I find myself giddy with anticipation at the prospect of such a promise! Against such things, who would argue?

However, I confess I don't spend many of my days eagerly looking forward to the great and glorious day of the Lord. Of course, I'm excited. Don't get me wrong. The bed-rock foundation of my faith rests in this place. However, I am often tempted to glance backward and believe the *real* abundance got lost long ago in the Garden of Eden, some-where between the flourishing tree of life and the serpent's deadly snare. Human nature caught a glimpse of the counter-feit glamour of what it might be like to gain complete control and lose the battle; forever chaining us to the brokenness of this fallen world.

When our family structure changed, I empathized with Lot's wife who looked back at her city turned rubble and promptly dissolved into a pillar of salt. Poor dear. I probably would have done the same thing. The past, full of "what-ifs" and "what-could've-beens" carries a sweet seduction. I've wondered what it might have been like for Kelel and Senait to avoid such grief. What if they would have been able to grow up in, what I assume, was the original plan for their lives — with their first family? What if our biological four-some had proceeded as planned in the temperature controlled comfort zone of our holy huddle?

What if...?

I can't say with any real certainty how life would have turned out for any of us. Could God have reached into their desperate circumstances and shined His light of provision and prosperity right there in Ethiopia? Absolutely. He could have done exactly that. To this day, there are amazing ministries and people on the ground in Ethiopia and all over the world, preaching the Good News, caring for widows and orphans, healing the sick, and for all intents and purposes, laying down their lives for the "one." Nevertheless in *this* case, in *our* case, that is not how God chose to intervene.

Once again, we sit in the mysterious crux of God's holy paradox. He loved each one of us to such a degree that His Spirit traversed time and space and land and sea — exemplifying light and piercing the darkness — to bring us together as a family. In Psalm 68:5-6, King David sings of God as *"father to the fatherless, protector of widows."* To this end, the Lord *"sets the lonely in families."* A piece of heaven's destiny for our motley crew meant hand-picking six broken shells and lovingly gluing them together into one mosaic, using the ethereal epoxy of the Holy Spirit, so we could grow.

Many times, in the world of adoption, it may be unclear to passersby that a particular family is blended through the choice of covenant commitment, either through marriage, adoption or both. I have friends whose hearts' desire was that their adopted child would look just like them and God tenderly honored those requests. In our family, however, this is obviously not the case. Any Joe Schmoe can recognize we were brought together in a different way. Understandably, the sheer fact that we don't resemble carbon copies of each other often elicits long stares and inquisitive eyebrows.

One day, as I watched Senait in her element (that is to say tumbling end over end on the gymnastics floor) another mom engaged me in conversation. Our chat started as many sideline mommy conversations do — with introductions, pleasantries, and the traditional, "Where do you live?" "Which child is yours?" and so forth. She proudly identified her daughter as the one in the red shorts and the blue tank-top, while I attempted to describe my youngest with the usual verbiage, knowing our mother/daughter connection was not so obvious to the naked eye.

"Oh, mine?" I said. "She's the one with the 100-watt-smile. Yep, that one there — in the rainbow leotard — with the eyeglasses. I see she's also rolling around like a rabid dog. Ha! I guess the other kids seem to enjoy it..." I chuckled behind a sheepish grin. This mother took one look at me and another glance at Senait. She didn't need to be a rocket scientist to figure out my daughter was adopted. After explaining that yes, we had adopted Senait and her older brother from Ethiopia, the woman turned to me and without batting an eyelash replied, "What made you decide to bark up that tree?"

I sat dumbfounded. Bark? Up that tree? I had never heard anyone put it quite that way. Granted, adoption might not be the call for every family. I get that. However, this brusque retort was a first for me. Honestly, I wasn't sure how to respond. We were talking about our *children* here, not a timeshare rental. Still too stunned to utter a coherent thought, I muttered something about having a heart for adoption and, after some thought and prayer we desired to expand our family in this way. I did add the word "prayer" in hopes that she would infer our belief system. Why was it so hard for me to just say, "God called us to this" and exit stage left with a mic drop? Gosh darn it, I don't know. At that time, if I had possessed even an ounce of perspective and wherewithal, I might have answered quite differently. My children are now grafted so deeply into the fiber of my soul that my mama bear's heart would do anything for them!

So, gymnastics mom, if you're reading this book, I would tell you the tree of which you speak is, to us, a tree of life. This tree has ushered us into perspectives of the Kingdom I don't think we would have experienced otherwise. The fruit it bears brings us more joy, growth and continuous beauty than we ever dreamed possible. God's tender love and mercy drew us to this tree. To eat of its fruit opens our eyes to a bit of heaven on earth. I would suggest the blended nature of our appearance, both inside and out, represents the delightfully diverse nature of God. We are now privy to something quite astounding — the redemptive work of our Heavenly Father who continues, time after time, to make all things new.

Many people smile in amazement and respect when they see our family together. "Oh, how wonderful!" they often observe. "These kids are so lucky to have you." Truth be told, this is such an awkward thing for me to hear, mostly because I don't fully agree. In fact, I would argue quite the contrary. I believe we are actually more blessed by them. Although it was difficult, if not impossible, to distinguish at the outset of this journey, beauty began to sprout from the ashes the moment we met. Now I look back, not with a sense of longing, but with a sense of reverence and awe.

Individual personalities are blossoming and growing into their God-crafted design. The blended nature of our family blesses me mind, body and soul. Reese navigates his birth-ordered role with deftness of heart. It is such a treat to watch him lead with honesty (arguably too much at times!) and integrity. Brynn continues to flourish in beauty and grace. She effortlessly floats between grown-up conversation and innocent play. Kelel has transformed into a unique Ethiopian-American butterfly before our very eyes. His sophisticated soul underwent a traumatic adjustment, but his Jesus-shaped heart has nestled its way right into ours. And Senait, what can I say about our cheeky little caboose? Her smile can light up an entire room in the same way she is capable of literally "lighting up" said room! There is no telling the paths our children will take. We may be raising a future engineer, teacher, stylist-to-the-stars and circus performer, but at the end of the day, my ultimate hope and prayer is that each one of them falls in step with whatever plans God has for them.

The risk of saying "yes" to God turned into the most amazing blessing. I can say adoption is the most challenging journey we've embarked on to date, but it's unequivocally the best. It wasn't until we stepped out in faith in order to partner with God that our eyes opened to the brand-new, knock-your-socks-off, initially overwhelming but ultimately more beautiful vantage point of His Kingdom than we had experienced before. When the Lord whispered this invitation into the depths of our hearts and graciously asked us to release our grasp on the known (which, incidentally, is exactly what Kelel and Senait had to do as well) and turn our "stuff" over to him, it was as if we began to live; I mean really, truly live for the first time. Now, I want even more. (Not necessarily more kids! Our quiver may be full. Although, I've learned to never say never...) Enough really isn't enough. Now I just want more of Him. I want to follow where He leads, wherever or whatever that may be.

Granted, I still have much to learn and experience. I am merely scratching the surface of His infinite grace. Much like the crowds that followed Jesus back in the day, I easily fall prey to the confusion and snares of this world. Just as Jesus approached those throngs of followers two thousand years ago, I believe He approaches us today. Mark 6:34 tells us that Jesus, upon returning to the shore after a brief time away, greeted by hordes of onlookers, *"stepped out of the boat, and he had compassion on them because they were like sheep without a shepherd."* What did Jesus do in response? *"He taught them many things..."* Oh, how I long to keep learning the many things of the Kingdom of God!

The Good Shepherd desires to teach His beloved sheep, to reveal to us the greatest treasure of all, His heart. When we dedicate intentional time and space to, not only reading His story, but experiencing it as well, we can fully expect the Lord will show up. He will reveal His timeless plan through the power of the Holy Spirit. When we worship to encounter Him in this way, we tug on the heart-strings of heaven, pulling down bits and pieces at a time. Jesus declares, *"I will give you the keys of the kingdom of heaven; whatever you bind on earth will be bound in heaven, and whatever you loose on earth will be loosed in heaven,"* (Matthew 16:19, TNIV). These keys open the doors of binding and loosing in a sort of holy exchange.

In the Sermon on the Mount Jesus calls His people to be "poor in spirit," which literally means to be "winded, without breath" — like you've just climbed a 14,000 foot mountain and couldn't possibly take another vertical step. (Or, in my case, like I've just carried all my whiny kids' ski gear from the parking lot to the base of the ski hill. Just like that.) Ironically, this is exactly how God wants us to approach life each and every day. Not whiny, but winded — at least in a spiritual sense. He wants us to live in such a way that we couldn't possibly take another step without His help. In order for His beauty to shine even brighter in us, we must put down the toddler mentality of "Me do it!" and embrace the fact that God wants to yoke up with us so we don't have to bear the burdens of this world alone. He is able to supernaturally infuse His breath into ours; His yoke brings wisdom, beauty, acceptance and love. God's yoke is perfectly fitted to embrace our curves. Lord knows this girl's got some of those!

Whether or not you have chosen to walk the road of life under the loving watch of the Good Shepherd, the invitation remains the same. Jesus wants us to "give all our worries and cares to [Him]," (1 Peter 5:7). Not some worries — all worries. Not just the ones at the bottom of the priority list (the ones that really don't matter anyway) but the great, big, huge ones at the top as well. Not just the ones involving other people's lives and other people's stuff, but the ones wrapped so tight around your tender heart you think you might explode from the pressure. Praying, "Thy will be done..." only feels palatable when you know that you know that you know the will of which we speak — the will of the Father — only manifests in tender compassion and radical, unconditional love. He sees the bigger picture and promises to redeem all things for good.

"Easy for *you* to say," you might be thinking. "You don't know what I'm going through. My life is hard. I don't see redemption of past hurts. I haven't experienced the victory you describe. I can barely _____ (fill in the blank!)_____ get up in the morning because I'm in so much pain/control an unruly child/make it through the day/look at my husband– let alone create intimacy with him/pay my mounting medical bills/overcome deep grief...." You name it, God wants it. He really, truly wants you to give it to Him, which means releasing control of the outcome and trusting Him to lead you in the way of wisdom down the particular path He has designed for you.

Just how, pray tell, does one give it all to Him? I honestly don't know any other way than to say this doesn't usually happen naturally. You can't muster enough fortitude and just give it the "old college try." You can't really give anything of value to God in your own strength. This process only happens in what I like to call, *"A Beautiful Exchange."*

Ever since I was a child, I have been fascinated with hot air balloons. In fact, each time I see a hot air balloon in the sky, or an image of one on a bumper sticker or dollar store t-shirt, I smile because I know God sees me; wherever I am, whatever I'm doing. The image of a hot air balloon immediately connects me with the supernatural. I call it a "God wink." This association between the presence of God and hot air balloons first came to me one summer as I sat criss-cross-applesauce alongside other 12-year-old girls in a rustic, wood cabin at Pioneer Girl camp.

As an early adolescent, I was more than a little green and quite wet behind the ears. Impressionable is an understatement. Even though I can't recall exact names and faces of the other girls in my cabin, I vividly remember the story. As was the routine each night during a week at camp, we huddled pajama-clad at the feet of our camp counselor. Before we giggled our way through lights out, we took time to discuss life and faith. We listened to each other's fragile stories and held them gingerly — wondering if it was safe enough share our own.

On one of these nightly soirees, our counselor shared about a time in her life when everything seemed to be going wrong. There was something about her husband being gravely ill, medical bills piled a mile high and God seemed all too distant. One day, she got into her car to go visit a trusted friend. She drove along the outskirts of town dazed and confused, when all of a sudden she looked up and saw a hot air balloon floating above the horizon. In that instant, God impressed a profound truth on her heart. The air in the car grew eerily still and she felt God say, *"Darling, you are like this hot air balloon. Even though I am invisible to you, I carry you. As this balloon floats, seemingly supernaturally, you rest in my tender arms. I will take care of you and provide for your every need."*

Our counselor's voice trailed off as she recounted that moment. She described how she shook her head and blinked her eyes, wondering if she'd actually heard the audible voice of God or just experienced a deep impression from Holy Spirit. She wasn't entirely sure. Nevertheless, she knew she heard or, at least, *felt* something out of the ordinary. She continued on her way, shaking her head in amazement. When she arrived at her destination, she walked in and her friend handed her a cup of coffee. She happily accepted the kind gesture and when she went to take her first sip, she noticed the mug she held in her hands displayed an image of a hot air balloon.

Later that same afternoon, as she absent-mindedly folded laundry in front of a daytime soap opera, something once ordinary became extraordinary. A commercial she would normally mute and dismiss hit her in an altogether different way that day because the company's logo and theme for the commercial was (you guessed it!) a hot air balloon. Images of hot air balloons continued to appear in the most random places. Each time she saw one from then on, she smiled and remembered the Lord's tender words to her in her time of need.

For some reason, I personally connected to that story and have garnered it as my own. Ever since that day, hot air balloons have become a symbol of God's love and care for me as well. Whenever I see one, my heart beats a little faster because I feel God's presence in that moment. It's like He's winking just at me.

Throughout the pages of this book, you have undoubtedly learned more than you ever cared to know about me and my idiosyncratic personality. However, I must confess one more thing. I am not a scientist, nor a mathematician. (Shocker!) In fact, my parents were so understanding and aware of this fact (a.k.a. my limitations and severe propensity to stress about such subjects), they allowed me to pick between Physics and Calculus my senior year of high school. Bless them for not requiring me to take both. I chose Physics. At least interesting scientific facts and principles accompany the confusing array of numbers — unlike Calculus, which continues to be a black hole of unintelligible symbols and letters in which I would get lost, never to be seen or heard from again.

Despite my utter lack of intelligence with mathematical or scientific know-how, there is actually one physical principle that intrigues me. This will come as no surprise — it's that of the hot air balloon. When I read the following description after a recent Google search on the science of hot air balloons, I couldn't help but draw a distinct parallel between the exchange of air used to propel a hot air balloon and the beautiful exchange between our natural selves and the supernatural working of the Holy Spirit. Here's what I found:

If you actually need to get somewhere, a hot air balloon is a fairly impractical vehicle. You can't really steer it, and it only travels as fast as the wind blows.

But if you simply want to enjoy the experience of flying, there's nothing quite like it. Many people describe flying in a hot air balloon as one of the most serene, enjoyable activities they've ever experienced. Hot air balloons are also an ingenious application of basic scientific principles...You'll be amazed by the beautiful simplicity of these early flying machines.

*Hot air balloons are based on a very basic scientific principle: **warmer air rises in cooler air.** Essentially, hot air is lighter than cool air because it has less mass per unit of volume.*

The article went on to map out all the mathematical mumbo jumbo, but the crux of it was this — "*to lift 1,000 pounds, you need about 65,000 cubic feet of hot air.* That's a lot of hot air! (Watch it...)

Of course I can't really wrap my mind around the numbers, but I am blown away (no pun intended) by the basic principle of this great exchange. Warm air rises and replaces cooler air. In the same way, God's Holy Spirit flows into our hearts and replaces the natural tendency of our fleshly self. The old retreats, allowing space for the new to come in. "*Those who are dominated by the sinful nature think about sinful things, but those who are controlled by the Holy Spirit think about things that please the Spirit. If your sinful nature controls your mind, there is death. But if the Holy Spirit controls your mind, there is life and peace,*" (Romans 8:5-6, NLT). There is no steering wheel on a hot air balloon. The balloon goes in whatever direction the wind blows. May the wind in our sails be that of God's Holy Spirit.

In God's economy, through the mysterious exchange of life and death we can, in fact, *exchange* our sinful nature for life and peace. The apostle Paul explains this very principle in Galatians 5, vs. 1 & 13, "*So Christ has really set us free.*

Now make sure that you stay free, and don't get tied up again in slavery and the law...For you have been called to live in freedom — not freedom to satisfy your sinful nature, but freedom to serve one another in love," (NLT).

Friends, I am perched on the tip of the iceberg here, kind of like a 15-year-old with a driver's permit, learning how to freely maneuver this beautiful truth. However, even in my relative infancy, the freedom found within this revelation has been and continues to be nothing short of radically life-changing. The supernatural love of Christ allows me to exchange offense for grace, bitterness for forgiveness, frustration for freedom, entitlement for gratitude, an attitude of "I-am-in-control" for a posture of "God-is-in-control." Channeling this beautiful exchange is indeed one of the most "serene, enjoyable activities" I have ever experienced.

While I admit I am a stubborn student, I am a grateful one. Even though my natural self often wants to settle for easy and comfortable, my mind and heart have expanded ever so slightly to allow the Holy Spirit a chance to speak — to offer a different way, a way that brings light and life and joy and peace. The phrase "Here I am, send me," no longer scares the ever-living daylights out of me. Well, let's be honest, sometimes it does, but now I see that natural risk, at the invitation of a loving God, comes packaged with supernatural reward. The *beautiful exchange* of heaven meeting earth starts where my *natural*, personal comfort zone ends and the *supernatural*, God-crafted journey begins.

Chapter 12:

Life in the "Splash Zone"

*"Today I have given you the choice between life
and death, between blessings and curses. I call on
heaven and earth to witness the choice you make.
Oh, that you would choose life, that you and your
decedents might live! Choose to love the LORD
your God and to obey him and commit yourself to
him, for he is your life..."*

— *Deuteronomy 30:19-20a, NLT*

S o this one time, Scott went to Sea World without me. Not
band camp — Sea World. Normally, I wouldn't deem this
kind of thing book worthy. I mean, it's not like he went to one
of the Seven Wonders of the World, but it's worth a mention
because this particular trip was different. You see, I had been
looking forward to this special getaway for four whole years!
Mind you, it's not that I had never been to Sea World. I have
"oohed" and "aahed" with hundreds of other over-heated tour-
ists at the dolphins' synchronized swim show and wondered if
I too might ride on the back of one of those majestic creatures
someday. Not likely, as I've since discovered. I've played

along as Clyde the sea lion and that rascally otter entertained the masses with their slapstick shenanigans.

No, it wasn't that I was a Sea World rookie. Rather, I wanted to go with Scott on this occasion because it was attached to a Young Life conference that's kind of like Haley's comet in its appearance. The Young Life All-Staff conference takes place in Orlando, Florida every four years in an effort to honor and celebrate the dedication and achievement of YL staff from around the world. At the time, Scott was in charge of the planning team and, as such, had a hand in coordinating the excursion to Sea World that was going to be a *surprise* gift for the nearly 4,000 folks in attendance. I was one of only a handful of people who actually knew about the surprise in advance.

During these extended weekend conferences, men and women of all shapes and sizes, tribes and tongue, gather for a much needed time of respite and communion with the Lord. Sounded great to me! Trust me when I say a corporate convening of Young Life staff puts even the most exuberant Disney worker's over-enthusiastic happy quotient to shame. Even if ministry life has beaten you down to a pulp, you wouldn't dare resign from the job before you had the chance to make it to at least one more all-staff conference. Young Lifers are always ready for a good time. So, when there's a pre-planned party just for them, you can bet it's gonna rock. I was *not* about to miss this one if I could help it.

There was just one little snafu. This particular conference was scheduled to take place four weeks after we brought our kids home from Ethiopia. Admittedly, not a great time to travel, but I still held some delusion of hope my mom might be able to come stay with the kids and I could sneak away for 48 hours. What could it hurt to be gone for only two days? However, the cog in the wheel, for which I did not account, surfaced when I discovered all four of my kids boasted a raging case of head lice! As such, I was off to

Walgreens — not Sea World. While I treated their scalps with RID, Listerine and mayonnaise (I desperately tried any and all remedies), I indulged in a different type of party. A party of the pity variety; for the love.

Now that some time has passed, we really can laugh about the insanity of those days. Kind of. I don't necessarily wish to repeat them, but the Lord truly redeemed the craziness in so many ways, not the least of which was coming to the rescue when a friend called me in an absolute panic after she realized her little brood was infested as well. Although, since Scott did not experience the privilege of participating in the lice brigade, I often release a sarcastic, "Ha!" when he sympathetically tries to connect with others battling those incessant bugs by saying "we too" have dealt with lice. (Yeah, kind of like "we too" have given birth.) In any event, Scott's smile broadens as he remembers what he got to be a part of during those days at the conference when he helped pull off the ultimate surprise party for those in attendance.

He says the giddiness was palpable that night as folks boarded dozens of charter buses set to take them straight to Sea World for a magical night under the stars. Surprised staff members stumbled into the park, full of happiness. The daytime crowd had dissipated and Young Life enjoyed the whole place to themselves. No lines — just fun. Husbands and wives rode and re-rode roller coasters until they were sick with delight. People filed in by the hundreds to fill Shamu's arena and watched in awe and wonder as Shamu did what he always does — thrill the crowd with gigantic jumps and tender kisses, all to the tune of adoring applause.

Perhaps you've been to Sea World, so you already know this, but when you enter the stadium you can decide one of two things. Well, three things. 1. Where to sit; 2. Who to sit next to; and; 3. Whether or not you'll splurge on an outrageously priced Sea World slushie in an obscenely large Shamu-shaped plastic cup. I pass no judgment whatsoever regarding your personal indulgence on point number three, but I do want to offer some reflections on the other two.

Choice Number 1: Where to Sit

You can play it safe and dry in the upper seats, where the delicate golf clap is a perfectly acceptable response to watching a trained killer whale show off his mad skills. That is a respectable choice, indeed. You are, after all, *at* the show. You aren't standing outside wondering what the heck is going on in there, furrowing your brow and inquiring about all the hootenanny within. In theory, you have at least chosen to enter the party and partake of the experience, albeit from a calculated distance. Your hairdo will most likely remain intact.

Then again, you could elbow your way right up to the front and plant yourself in the designated "splash zone," where the magnitude of applause and frivolity is off the chain! However, if you sit in the splash zone you are guaranteed at least one thing. You will get wet. No doubt about it. And by wet, I mean completely drenched. You're likely to compromise your hairdo and your outfit as well, but you would also likely position yourself to whole-heartedly experience the show in all its intended extravagance.

This over-the-top experience was probably the express intent the architects had in mind when they designed the stadium. Scott purports the people who outwardly expressed the most joy that night were the ones who chose to sit in the splash zone. Doubled over with laughter, their smiles radiated from ear to ear as they exited the park.

I believe the analogy of the splash zone translates into a broader perspective and embodies a wonderful metaphor for how we can choose to approach life. Granted, everything we face — each circumstance, every experience — isn't necessarily going to entertain us like Shamu does at Sea World. Often times the context of our reality may be far from fun. In fact, it may be downright nightmarish, but we can wake up every morning and choose how close we want to sit to the splash zone of life. How close we want to be to the action. The nearer we are, the greater the possibility we will get drenched, but we will also position ourselves to live life to the absolute fullest which is, after all, one of the very reasons Jesus came (John 10:10) in the first place.

Choice Number 2: Who to Sit Next to

Choosing who to sit next to in any area of life, whether it be in the boardroom or at the breakfast table, is a human dilemma as old as the social stratosphere represented by the school cafeteria itself. Even now, beads of sweat pool on my brow as I remember how the brown plastic tray shook in my hands when I stared at the sea of tables in the middle school cafeteria. Everyone seemed to be paired up with an adoring BFF and I was the only one paralyzed by fear and indecision. Where I sat and with whom could make the difference between overnight popularity or social suicide. In some ways, I relive this experience from time to time through the eyes of my own children.

When I drive them home from school, I frequently hunt for connecting points that might help me glean any inkling of insight into their day. The routine question, "How was your day?" rolls off the tongue with ease, but generally elicits the same easily regurgitated response in the form of a deep, guttural grunt. Although sometimes, if I'm really lucky, I receive an actual verbal reply to the tune of, "It was fine..." Three whole words. Wow. These less than stellar responses have led me to resort to a different tactic altogether in order to earn more than a trite answer. I dive head first into the tumultuous waters of schoolyard relationships. Many times the questions that siphon out genuine compound sentences, boil down to these: "Who did you play with at recess?" and "Who did you sit next to at lunch?" The answers to these questions actually reveal more to me than my kids may realize about their world-view. Who my children voluntarily spend time with tells me a lot about who they are as well as who they *want* to be. (Or at least, who they want to be like.)

Now, I am not suggesting we go through life only playing with and sitting next to the people we like best to the exclusion of others. On the contrary. If we are serious about following Jesus' model for relationship, we are called to engage with the poor, the downtrodden and the broken-hearted. The ones on the margins. The ones sitting alone in the cafeteria of life. Sometimes these people are naturally likable characters and sometimes, relating to folks that are different than us is downright uncomfortable. Nevertheless Jesus, being the kind of guy who hung out with *all* types of people, makes it clear He's not too worried about our personal comfort. He is far more interested in the motivation and connection of our heart with His and with those around us. The Holy Spirit might just want us to get comfortable with being uncomfortable.

However, as much as Jesus ministered to the marginalized and overlooked, He also surrounded himself with close friends and followers. Although He loved everyone equally (so much so He voluntarily went to the cross for all mankind), He also chose to sit next to a smaller crew of men and women who understood His heart; the ones whose hearts and minds represented fertile soil. Often, after Jesus spoke to the masses, He pulled His disciples aside to give them extra nuggets of revelation and wisdom saved just for them. He knew few would understand His mission, but to those who did, He offered intimate revelation about the Kingdom of God. As such, Jesus' motley band of misfits gave up everything they had to take up their crosses and follow Him.

Who are we going to choose to sit next to in this thing called life? With whom will we share our real heart? What type of people will we "do" life with? Do we want to ally

ourselves with others safely perched in the nose-bleed section? People who bow to the gods of image and worldly success? May I suggest that striving after such things will only
lead to a rather dry and tepid temporal existence? *Or* do
we want to take a chance and experience the "splash zone"
along with the type of people who don't mind getting sop-
ping wet and living life to the fullest? The ones who are doubled over in laughter and awe because they are looking for
and following the movement of the Spirit and, in so doing,
frequently find themselves turning to each other in holy awe,
with mouths agape saying, "What in the world? Did you just
see that?! God *really* is that good!"

In her own words, writer Anne Lamott describes a key
component necessary for anyone actively living in the splash
zone when she writes, *"To participate requires self-discipline
and trust and courage, because this business of becoming
conscious… is ultimately about asking yourself, as [her]
friend Dale puts it, 'How alive am I willing to be?'"*

How alive are you willing to be? How alive am I willing
to be? How alive are *we* willing to be?

That's the question I asked myself at the outset of this
journey — this journey that led to an adoption, which led
to deep soul-searching, which led to letting go of my naturally selfish flesh in order to live into the Spirit-led life. The
Spirit-led life is the true treasure. The treasure is also knowing
that God's greater story shines above and around, inside and
in spite of my own. I believe this type of treasure is like
a lighthouse. Again, Lamott wisely observes, *"Lighthouses
don't go running all over an island looking for boats to save;
they just stand there shining."*

Lighthouses steadfastly shine light to those around them.
Shining light is their express and only job. Running hel-
ter-skelter is not at all the way to uncover the greatest treasure on heaven and earth. Rather, leaning into the hands of
the One who molded us and finding our truest identity in

Him is how to find the "x" that marks the spot. Living in the Kingdom of God is like settling into the ultimate splash zone; into the place where full, abundant, hairdo-wrecking life is found. Yes, it's risky. Yes, it's unpredictable. In the oft quoted words of popular British author, CS Lewis, it is *"not safe — but it is good."*

To live in the splash zone of the Kingdom is not always safe. In fact, many times it is downright unpredictable and quite dangerous, but it is always good. To begin living in this zone has taken me to places outside my comfort zone I never dreamed of, but like a toddler thrown high in the air by her strong and mighty father, it takes my breath away. I want to shout, "Again, Daddy! Do it again!" I want to take Jesus' hand and do it again. I don't necessarily mean adoption — I'm pretty sure we're done expanding our family. (Right, God?! Although, I suppose stranger things have happened...) Whatever the call, whether big or small, I want to live with open hands, ready to receive what the Lord has for me. I pray that God, in His mercy, will exchange more of my heart for His.

Lamott continues, *"We are given a shot at dancing with, or at least clapping along with the absurdity of life, instead of being quashed by it over and over again. It's like singing on a boat during a terrible storm at sea. You can't stop the raging storm, but singing can change the hearts and spirits of the people who are together on that ship."*

So, what do you say? Shall we sing together in the splash zone of the ship of life? Lord willing, our collective song will be so loud the sound of it will spritz love and blessing on all those who choose to sit near enough to hear. I, for one, don't want to rest until the reality of this engulfs my very being. Granted, I may spend the rest of my life taking baby steps, but thank the Lord there is grace for that!

Missionary Frank Laubach offers words to my search in a prayer he wrote on the first day of January, 1937...

155

"God, I want to give you every minute of this year. I shall try to keep you in mind every moment of my waking hours... I shall try to let you be the speaker and direct every word. I shall try to let you direct my acts. I shall try to learn your language.'"

There it is. I shall try. Perhaps the most profound grace exists in the brave act of simply trying. Smack in the center of the hard and the good and the exciting and the mundane — right in the middle of the washing and the folding and the working and the praying and the playing — we simply lift our eyes to catch another view. A view of something different, something bigger than ourselves; a view that beckons us to step outside our comfort zone and try something new. For the sake of the call — for the good of us all.

It may not be easy. Most likely it won't. But it will be good. Yes, it will be good! Besides, the shortest distance between two points is rarely very interesting. Wouldn't you agree?

So — there you have it. What do you say? Will you extend your arm and take His hand while He gently leads the long way 'round?

THE LONG WAY 'ROUND

The gate beckons, gleaming bright
To enter its haven just seems

Right.

Predictable gardens of comfort bloom within
Surely this leads to the race I am to win.

How simple it appears to be
To pick the lock and enter thee.

I imagine a future within your walls
My thoughts dance freely through palatial halls.

My hand extends and then

I pause

A faint whisper invites another cause.

What's that? A voice? I see no man.
It's nothing I reason, just stick with the plan.

Try as I might, I cannot shake
The feeling there is a sweeter path to take.

It makes no sense! The gate is near
The breadth made wide for all to clear.

Why would I choose the narrow way?
The world's nectar begs me stay.

And yet

I sense if I tarry there

I will miss a pearl all too rare.
Fighting against the flesh of my being

I turn and take a step without seeing.
Uncertainty looms, but does not overcome.

Light shines on the joy of His glorious drum.
Even for this wretch His grace abounds
As He gently leads
The long way 'round.

— *Megan Nilsen*

157

Personal Reflection / Small Group Discussion Questions

> *"I love the man that can smile in trouble, that can gather strength from distress, and grow brave by reflection. 'Tis the business of little minds to shrink, but he whose heart is firm, and whose conscience approves his conduct, will pursue his principles unto death."*

> — *Thomas Paine*

Dear Reader,

Perhaps you are the type of person who likes to experience something and ponder it in your heart. You don't necessarily feel the need to hop up and post every single, solitary thought on social media. You might read this book and absorb these words in a very personal and introspective way. Maybe you find the best person to process life with is — you! If so, you have my complete and utter blessing to go and do just that.

However, I suspect there are others of you who are more like me. You are verbal processors through and through. You cannot rest until you get that thing inside you that must be shared out into the open, either in a private journal only to be seen by you and the Lord Himself, or with others — through your blog, over a good cup of coffee or even within the confines of safe and challenging small group discussion.

Whatever the case, I offer a few questions you can refer to for personal reflection or small group discussion throughout the course of this book. These are questions that came to my mind as I wrote. Quite frankly, these are questions the Lord continues to ask me even now. As such, I humbly offer them to you as well.

If we want to grow into brave, faith-filled, inspired individuals (as Thomas Paine suggests), it is important to reflect on our lives. Once we look back to see where we've been, we may better understand where we are and, ultimately, chart the course to see where we are going. I strongly believe your journey will be better for it!

Feel free to discuss all or none of the questions below... They are yours.

Introduction: In the Beginning, Once Upon a Time and All That Jazz
1. What does your faith journey look like? How has it grown or changed over the years?
2. Have you ever said "yes" to a divine invitation? If so, what was it? How did it change your life?
3. How would you describe your spiritual satisfaction? Are you content or hungry for more of God? Why or why not?
4. What does the phrase "Kingdom of God" mean to you?

Chapter 1: "God, Send Me" and Other Things We Might Not *Really* Mean
1. Are you intrigued by the thought of living into a bigger story? What might that look like?
2. How do you determine if a "call" is from God? What does it mean to have His anointing?

3. What does it mean/look like for God to use you for His purposes – whether large or small? How are you tempted to put your own personal parameters around each/ every task?

4. Reflect on the Oswald Chambers quote, "The call of God is not for the special few, it is for everyone. Whether or not I hear God's call depends upon the state of my ears; and what I hear depends upon *my* disposition." How do you react to this statement? How would you describe your current disposition?

5. Do you relate with Megan's confession, "Really, God? Are you sure you have the right people? If we take a step off the cliff with you, Jesus, will we free fall or will we fly?" Have you ever felt this way? Describe a time you questioned God and doubted His goodness.

6. How do you feel about change? Do you welcome it or shy away from it? How has your attitude towards change affected your life?

Chapter 2: Beach Entry Exploration Outside the "Comfort Zone"

1. Have you ever been discontent in a certain season of life? Were you tempted to dream of a rosier future?

2. Do you sense God stirring an alternate reality or change in your life at the moment? If so, what feelings, excitement or reservation does that bring?

3. Megan quit her long-awaited job because she sensed God calling her to be available to whatever new thing He might have for their family. In what ways might God be calling you to be obedient or make a hard decision, even if you don't exactly know why?

4. How do you discern if these thoughts of change/obedience are from God or figments of your own mind?

5. Are there any thoughts or dreams you are carrying around in secret? Do you feel a nudge from the Lord

to share these with others? If so, with whom? How would sharing this free you?

Chapter 3: Following God is Like a Box of Chocolates

1. Has God ever called you to do something that terrified you? If so, how did you respond?
2. How do you know whether to step out in faith or wait for further instruction?
3. Have you ever received a word or impression from the Lord? What was it like? How did you know it was Him?
4. What things feel comfortable to you right now? How might God be calling you out of your comfort zone and into a bigger story? What's the difference between something *nice* and something *more*?
5. Do you ever wish you could see into the future? How might the ability to do so hamper your faith experience?

Chapter 4: Lost in Translation

1. How do you like to communicate with others?
2. Describe a time you misunderstood someone or you felt misunderstood. How did that feel?
3. What feelings did this chapter bring up in you?
4. As you identify these feelings, what will you do with them? Be specific.

Chapter 5: Grief — a Four-Letter Word

1. Megan opens with the CS Lewis quote, "No one ever told me that grief felt so much like fear." What does this mean to you? How are fear and grief intertwined in the Nilsen's preliminary months as a family of six? Are you or a loved one currently experiencing any feelings of grief? If so, how are you processing those feelings?

2. How do you navigate conversations with kids or other loved ones when they are scared? What do you do if you are scared, too? Relate an example if you can. What did you learn from that?

Chapter 6: An Inconvenient Truth — *We Are Both*
1. What do you think of Brene Brown's quote at the top of this chapter? What are some of the greatest barriers to your own connection with other people?
2. How do you feel about asking others for help? Is it easier for you to offer help or receive it?
3. Have you ever felt called by God to do something but, after saying yes, the reality of answering the call felt too big, heavy, or sad to endure for any length of time? If so, what did you do or what are you doing?
4. Describe a time in the past when you felt stuck or without hope. How did you react and how did it alter your view of God or the circumstance?
5. Why do you suppose Megan says vulnerability is the key to breakthrough? What might that look like? What do you think is the key to spiritual and emotional breakthrough?
6. What does Psalm 34:17-19 say about achieving breakthrough?
7. How does great anguish usher us into the heart of God? Do you believe this to be true? Can you give an example?

Chapter 7: "Motherhood is Not Your Greatest Calling..."
1. How does the phrase, "Motherhood is not your greatest calling" sit with you? Instead of "motherhood," what word would you insert here that would relate to your life?
2. What kind of greater community do you have in your life? Do you have friends, family, or a therapist to

help shed light on your struggles or what Megan
refers to as her "darker demons?" What might you
identify as those in your own life?

3. What defines you? In what or in who do you find your
   identity?
4. Have you ever felt lost or hidden — like you weren't
   your true self?
5. What does it mean/look like to find your identity in
   Jesus? What questions does this raise for you?
6. What stumbling blocks continue to trip you up from
   living like a child of the King 100% of the time?
7. In what ways are you tempted to put your worth or
   identity in the world? How might you find peace and
   freedom focusing on the process rather than the outcome — allowing God to refine you along the way?

Chapter 8: Corruption Ain't Just a River in Washington, D.C.
1. What does it mean when Megan says, "However great
   our works and deeds appear, they are but clanging
   gongs if they lack genuine love"? How does this statement challenge your faith?
2. How do you navigate present circumstances with the
   hope of a future heaven?
3. How are you tempted to be ruled by your emotions?
   Can you give an example?
4. Can obedience to God actually uncover corruption of
   heart? Why or why not?
5. Why do you think Scott felt like the rich young ruler?
   Can you relate to him in any way?

Chapter 9: The Issue with Identity Issues
1. Are you currently receiving all God has for you as
   His beloved child? Why or why not?

2. Describe a time you made a decision out of fear or people-pleasing. What was the outcome? How did you feel afterwards?
3. Do you believe, as Megan suggests, that breakthrough can be directly linked to obedience to and honesty with God? What is your response to this?
4. How does the fact that you are child/heir of God have the potential to change everything? What does that look like for you?
5. What dreams has God laid on your heart? How does knowing you are His child change your perspective and potential action in regard to those dreams?
6. How can you tell if your choices/actions/responses smell of fear or speak of love?

Chapter 10: Redemption Song
1. Open some of the windows of testimony in your own life. Where has God met you in your hour of need and provided redemption to some of the harder parts of your story?
2. What are your thoughts about, or experiences with, spiritual warfare? How do you distinguish between the natural and the spiritual realm?
3. Megan confesses that her insatiable need to control her children plagues her more often than she'd care to admit. What challenges frequently surface for you? How do you tackle those issues or skirt them altogether?
4. What does it look like to have peace in spite of your circumstances? Who do you know that models this well?
5. What unique assignments do you believe God has for you? For what kind of God-shaped adventure do you sense Him preparing you?

6. If God calls you to a smaller or less visible role — yet important in His Kingdom — would you be okay with that? Does it feel less exciting? Explain. Can you say, "Whatever call you give me, I will gladly obey"?

Chapter 11: On Earth as it is in Heaven (a.k.a. A Beautiful Exchange)
1. In what ways has the Good Shepherd pursued you as His beloved sheep like He pursues "the one"?
2. What risk might God be asking you to take in order to experience a little more heaven here on earth?
3. What worldly worries is Jesus asking you to release to Him, even now?

Chapter 12: Life in the "Splash Zone"
1. Have you ever had to miss out on something you were really looking forward to? What happened and how did you feel?
2. What types of things or people make you uncomfortable? How do you navigate relationships and experiences outside your comfort zone?
3. What does the phrase, "Comfortable with being uncomfortable" mean to you? How might God be using the "uncomfortable" to strengthen or deepen your faith?
4. With what type of people are you "doing life"? How does your immediate community shape your worldview and life experience? Is there anything you would change about where you're "sitting" and with whom?
5. How alive are you willing to be? Are you hungry to live a bigger story? What does/might that look like for you?
6. Journal your heart responses to the Lord here or in a separate notebook. Pay attention to the thoughts and feelings God puts on your heart. Ask Him to grant

wisdom or clarity regarding anything you write down. If you feel so led, share these thoughts/dreams with a trusted friend. Lay them at the Lord's feet and see how He picks them up and moves you forward into His divine plan for your life.

Press on, friend and go with God! You may be challenged beyond what you think you can handle, but if you link your yoke with His you will not be disappointed. Let's exchange our plans for His plans, our fleshly inclinations for His supernatural grace and love. I am thankful for you and I pray for you as you embark on a journey of divine proportions. May you fully and bravely enter the story written just for you. A story that will lead you – home. Let's do this thing!

Bibliography:

Introduction:
Jack Deere, *Surprised by the Voice of God*, Grand Rapids, Michigan: Zondervan Publishing, 1996

Chapter 1: "Here am I! Send Me" and Other Things We Might not *Really* Mean
Oswald Chambers, *My Utmost for His Highest*, Grand Rapids, Michigan: Discovery House Publishers, 1935, p. 8
Sarah Young, *Jesus Calling*, Nashville, Tennessee: Thomas Nelson, 2004

ESV Bible Translations

Chapter 4: Lost in Translation
CS Lewis, *The Magician's Nephew*, Harper Collins Publishing, reprint 1994

Chapter 5: Grief — a Four-Letter Word
CS Lewis, *A Grief Observed*, Harper One, 1 edition 2009

Chapter 6: An Inconvenient Truth — *We Are Both*
Brené Brown, *The Gifts of Imperfection: Let Go of Who You Think You're Supposed to Be and Embrace Who You Are*, Hazelden Publishing, 2010

Frank Laubach, *Practicing His Presence*, printed by Seed Sowers Publishing, Jacksonville, Florida, pg 10

Chapter 8: Corruption Ain't Just a River in Washington, D.C.
Frank Laubach, *Practicing His Presence*, pg. 6-7

Greek word translations, www.BlueLetterBible.org

Emily P. Freeman, *A Million Little Ways: Uncover the Art You Were Made to Live*, Grand Rapids, MI: Revell, 2013, p.26

Chapter 9: The Issue with Identity Issues
Heather Forbes & B. Bryan Post, *Beyond Consequences, Logic and Control: A Love-Based Approach to Helping Children with Severe Behaviors*, Boulder, CO: Beyond Consequences Institute, LLC, 2009, pp. xi-xii, 3, 13-14

Chapter 10: Redemption Song
Frank Laubach, *Practicing His Presence*, pg. 1

Christine Caine, IF:Gathering, February 2014

Francis Frangipane, *The Three Battlegrounds*, Cedar Rapids, IA: Arrow Publications, 1989, pp. 52 & 48

Christine Caine, www.christinecaine.com, quoted from her 'first things first' daily email, dated 12/31/2014

Chapter 11: On Earth as it is in Heaven (a.k.a. A Beautiful Exchange)
How Stuff Works, http://science.howstuffworks.com/transport/flight/modern/hot-air-balloon.htm

Frank Laubach, *Practicing His Presence*, pp. 22-23, 26

Chapter 12: Living in the "Splash Zone"
Anne Lamott, *Bird by Bird*, New York, NY: Random House, Inc, pp. 236 & 237

Frank Laubach, *Prayer: The Mightiest Force in the World*, Old Tappan, NJ, Fleming H. Revell Company, MCMXLVI, MCMLIX

To find more information about ministries on the ground in Ethiopia helping widows and orphans and sharing the Gospel of God's great love, as well as others mentioned in this book, you can visit the following websites:

Bring Love In — http://bringlove.in

All God's Children International — http://allgodschildren.org

Show Hope – http://showhope.org

Encourage Africa — www.encourageafrica.com

Young Life — http://www.younglife.org

Mothers of Preschoolers — http://mops.org

Author Bio:

Megan Nilsen is the mother of four children–two biological, two adopted, and by all accounts the most beautiful kids in the world (at least according to their unbiased mother). She is married to her college sweetheart who inspires her everyday to be the woman God made her to be. Together, they believe the local church is the hope of the world. When she's not coordinating crazy carpool schedules, she rejuvenates as part of the teaching team for her women's Bible study. Megan passionately pursues writing as a way to process God's ever-active work in the world and gets the biggest rush out of connecting with people and swapping stories of the heart. She and her family live in Colorado. You can find her blogging about it all with two of her dearest friends at **www.writingin-pencil.com** or follow her on Twitter: @mbnilsen

CPSIA information can be obtained
at www.ICGtesting.com
Printed in the USA
FSOW02n1906260615
8324FS